THE LIFE OF DESIDERIUS ERASMUS

The life of Desiderius Erasmus

by

ALBERT HYMA

Professor Emeritus of History
University of Michigan

VAN GORCUM & COMP. N.V., ASSEN, 1972
DR. H. J. Prakke & H. M. G. Prakke

© 1972 by Koninklijke Van Gorcum & Comp. N.V., Assen, The Netherlands

No parts of this book may be reproduced in any form by print, photoprint, microfilm or any other means without written permission from the publisher

ISBN 90 232 0964 8

Printed in the Netherlands by Royal VanGorcum Ltd.

Preface

During the Erasmus Symposium at Ithaca College on October 27-28, 1969, the present writer made two pleasant discoveries. In the first place, a Japanese-American professor told him that there was set up by Dutch traders in Nagasaki a statue, which for a long time was considered to be that of the Buddha. But when finally a layer of film at the top was removed, the inscription indicated that the statue represented Erasmus of Rotterdam. This was not surprising, for one of the first Dutch ships to enter the harbor of Nagasaki was from Rotterdam, and its first name was Erasmus. In the second place, one of the two volumes being used in the local history department to cover the history of civilization had on its front cover the picture of Erasmus! No wonder that the leading Erasmus Symposium held in the United States of America had to be held in Ithaca, where the best biography of Erasmus thus far had been composed by Professor Preserved Smith.

It was also on the campus of Ithaca College that the author first conceived the plan to write a biography of Erasmus. His own lecture on Erasmus devoted a considerable amount of space to Preserved Smith, who in the year 1932 published in *The American Historical Review* a review of the writer's book entitled, *The Youth of Erasmus*. One day the writer saw a copy of the issue involved in the reading room of the Royal Library in Brussels, with the title of the review article on its front cover. This made the writer feel both proud and sentimental.

ALBERT HYMA

Contents

PREFACE		7
I.	BIRTH AND EARLY CHILDHOOD	9
II.	WITH THE BRETHREN OF THE COMMON LIFE	14
III.	AT THE MONASTERY OF STEYN	22
IV.	THE BOOK AGAINST THE BARBARIANS	31
V.	AT THE UNIVERSITY OF PARIS	37
VI.	THE FIRST TRIP TO ENGLAND	43
VII.	LIFE IN PARIS AND THE LOW COUNTRIES	51
VIII.	THE LONDON REFORMERS	59
IX.	THE GRAND TOUR OF ITALY	68
X.	THOMAS MORE AND ERASMUS	74
XI.	PROFESSOR AT CAMBRIDGE	80
XII.	THE GREEK NEW TESTAMENT	88
XIII.	LOUVAIN VERSUS WITTENBERG	93
XIV.	THE COLLOQUIES	105
XV.	CONVERSION	122
XVI.	ON THE SEPARATION OF STATE AND CHURCH	134

CHAPTER I

Birth and Early Childhood

Erasmus was born in the night of October 27-28, 1469. According to Melanchthon his birth occurred four hours before sunrise, or about 3 A.M. Erasmus mentioned the "eve of October 28;" hence it is safe to say that the event took place during the night.¹ As for the year of his birth, the most reliable reference is that published on p. 6 of the program issued in 1969 by the municipal government of Rotterdam.² This body had received its information from the Royal Dutch Academy of Sciences. Moreover, the celebrations held in honor of Erasmus in Louvain, Rotterdam, Brussels, Antwerp, Ghent, Liège, and Tours all favored the year 1969 for the programs issued; while the Erasmus Symposium held at Ithaca, N.Y. on October 27 and 28 also set the date at 1469. No reliable authority any longer dares to refute the chief authorities in The Netherlands and Belgium. The present writer in his book on young Erasmus, issued in 1931 and again in 1968, has presented important facts with which to establish the exact date he set forth as early as in 1930.

Erasmus in his famous autobiography entitled, *Compendium Vitae,* said that he "was born in Rotterdam on the eve of the festival of Simon and Jude, 57 years ago." It was composed in 1524. P.S. Allen in his marvelous edition of Erasmus' letters informs us in Volume I, pp. 46 and 575-578 that the statements of Erasmus "are correct even in small points." That, however, is not the case. For example, Erasmus reported this about his father: "The latter was secretly united with Margaret, in the hope of marriage. And there are some who say that the expectation was mutual, which greatly displeased the parents and brothers of Gerard, who hoped to make of him a priest." But the truth is that Gerard was

¹ A. Hyma, *The Youth of Erasmus,* both 1931 and 1968 editions, p. 51.
² Here we read this: "Ofschoon over Erasmus' geboortejaar geen eenstemming bestaat, zijn gewichtige argumenten aangevoerd voor de opvatting dat hij in 1469 het levenslicht zag."

9

already a priest before Erasmus was born, unknown to Allen and other British historians.

Our best original source on the birth of Erasmus is a note in a learned work by Cornelius Loos of Gouda, who was for many years a prominent citizen in that city. The title of his book was *Illustrium Germaniae Scriptorum Catalogus*. In the article on Erasmus he said this: "Prodiit in lucem anno 1469." When in the year 1555 the home for old men was founded, he became one of the three regents, as indicated by the present writer in his book on young Erasmus. Loos argued that the guilty father, who lived near Gouda, sent his servant to a neighboring city, meaning no doubt Rotterdam. The present writer in his biography presented a plate facing p. 52, showing the front of the house in which, according to tradition, Erasmus was born. Nearly all contemporary writers referred to him as Erasmus of Rotterdam. In the Nauwe Kerkstraat in Rotterdam there stands a house today giving a description to the effect that on this spot the great scholar was born.

The latter was always greatly disturbed when any reference was made to his birth. He decided from the beginning to cast a veil over the actual facts. This was particularly the case when in the year 1513 he was asking Pope Julius II for a dispensation which would remove the stain of his father's guilt. Consequently, the kind pontiff stated that Erasmus was the son of "a bachelor and a widow."[1] This embarrassing development has been overlooked by those scholars who in recent years have sought to establish Erasmus as the author of a scurrilous work entitled, *Julius Excluded*. Although the present writer has devoted an essay to the subject which was published in front of his *The Youth of Erasmus*, there are still some theologians and historians who continue to claim that Erasmus not only wrote that wretched dialogue but also a poem in which the poor pope was badly abused. Professor James D. Tracy in an article published in *Renaissance Quarterly* indicates that Wallace K. Ferguson, Craig R. Thompson, and E. Harris Harbison ignored a large work by Carl Stange on the authorship of *Julius Exclusus*, which we now must mention.[2] Some of the arguments used by these and other recent

[1] See A. Hyma, *The Youth of Erasmus*, p. 53.
[2] R. H. Bainton has also committed some astonishing errors in this direction. See especially his work entitled, *Erasmus of Christendom* (New York: Charles Scribners', 1969), pp. 14 and 16; James D. Tracy, "Erasmus Becomes a German", *Renaissance Quarterly*, Vol. 21 (1968), p. 286; A. Hyma, The *Youth of Erasmus*, pp. V-XII. See also a fascinating work entitled, *The Julius Exclusus of Erasmus*, containing a translation by Paul Pascal and an introduction by J. Kelley Sowards (Bloomington: Indiana University Press, 1968). Here we are informed that Erasmus was the author of an epigram against Julius II.

scholars must seem incredible to those who are actually familiar with the major works of Erasmus.

The name given to the little boy was from the beginning Erasmus, and not a Dutch equivalent. The father was no doubt a scholar, for Erasmus said that in Rome he diligently applied himself to the study of Latin and Greek.[1] And so he chose the Greek name Erasmus, while the additional name Desiderius was added by himself later on. For example, he issued a colloquy in the year 1522, introducing two speakers named respectively Erasmus and Desiderius. It was entitled, *Ars Notoria*, or *The Notorious Art*. Here follow a few lines: "Erasmus. I understand that there is a sort of art that enables a person to learn without any effort at all the liberal arts. Desiderius. What do you mean?" The editions of the *Colloquies* beginning in the year 1522 were dedicated to Johannes Erasmius Froben, who was the son of Johann Froben, Erasmus' main publisher after the year 1517. Later on Jerome Froben, the son of Johann Froben, acted as his principal publisher. In a poem addressed to the great scholar Gaguin in 1497, Erasmus called himself Desyderius Herasmus Rotterodamensis. He retained the name Herasmus until 1503, while the name Roterodamus was first used in 1506.[2]

On p. 19 we read this astonishing statement by Professor Sowards: "Like the Julius it was never claimed by Erasmus and was not published in his lifetime. Indeed it was brought to light only a generation ago by the French scholar J. B. Pineau, who, on a suggestion of P. S. Allen, discovered it in a manuscript copy in Erasmus' own hand." Moreover, in 1957 another copy was found by Cornelis Reedijk, and Sowards has indicated our source of information: "Een Schimpdicht van Erasmus op Julius II," published in *Opstellen door Vrienden en Collegas Aangeboden aan Dr. F. K. H. Kossmann* (The Hague, 1958), pp. 186-207. Sowards assumes that Erasmus was the author, which is a hazardous assumption on his part. In the first place, if Erasmus had written this work, there would have followed a terrific repercussion, merely because he was the author. And in the second place, Erasmus would have, undoubtedly, mentioned it in a later work, as was the case with that notorious colloquy, which discussed the futile attempt made by Pope Julius II to enter heaven. If one examines the contents of *Julius Exclusus* with care, he could not help but conclude that Erasmus, who had been greatly favored by the pope, would not have been so naive as to write: "Caesar had no greater compunction than do you about breaking his plighted word." Caesar despised the gods, and "are you not a Julius in this respect?" We must note here in this connection that Caesar's first name was Julius. The scurrilous poem continues as follows: "You differ from him in only one Tiny detail that, being of common stock, you love wine more than literature." At this point Sowards says that "this epigram is one of the most important links in the argument for Erasmus' authorship of the *Julius exclusus*." On the contrary, it is nothing of the sort! Erasmus was far too clever to indulge in such hazardous attacks on the man who had enabled him to obtain so many valuable favors.

[1] A. Hyma, *The Youth of Erasmus*, p. 55.
[2] P. S. Allen, *Opus Ep. Er.*, Vol. I, p. 73, first footnote.

When in the year 1517 Erasmus obtained from Pope Leo X a dispensation, he was addressed by the pontiff as follows: "Erasmo Rogerii Roterodamensi clerico." We may assume that Erasmus was then in no position to mislead Leo X into addressing him under the name of his own father, and so he chose that of his mother instead.[1] P.S. Allen unfortunately argued that Erasmus' father was named Rogerius Gerardus, for which reason he chose to use it to his own advantage in asking Leo X for a dispensation.[2] But we must not overlook the fact that Erasmus was trying to overcome the disadvantage of being the son of a Roman Catholic priest and his housekeeper. The pope in 1517 stated that Erasmus was the offspring of a damned and incestuous union.[3] Moreover, he had also been guilty of refusing to return to his monastery of Steyn, near Gouda. It is no wonder that he often hurled invectives at the leading monks, as we shall observe later on. Particularly bitter were his attacks upon the learned professors at the University of Paris, which we shall also discuss with some concern.

Let us then investigate with great care what caused Erasmus at the age of 28 to issue his bold attack upon scholasticism. First of all we must continue to examine his career before 1497, in order to determine just why certain traits of character were developed which naturally shaped his course of action. The fact that his father, Gerard, was a priest in the Roman Catholic Church and that his mother, Margaret, was this priest's housekeeper cast a terrible shadow upon his whole career. Margaret, as is well known, fled from Gouda, where she had been living, to her mother's home in Rotterdam. Consequently, her second son called himself Erasmus of Rotterdam. The older son was known as Peter. We do not know how long the mother waited in Rotterdam before returning to Gouda, but we do know that Erasmus was first taught in Gouda by a capable tutor and clergyman named Peter Winckel, who was the vice-rector of St. John's Church. He was probably born in the year 1469, and he was taught by Winckel from 1473 to 1475.[4]

When he was six years old Erasmus' father began to wonder where his younger son should attend a regular school. Gerard was well aware that in Gouda there was not a satisfactory school available at the time,

[1] A. Hyma, op. cit., p. 55.
[2] A. Hyma, op. cit., pp. 55-56.
[3] Preserved Smith, *Erasmus A Study of His Life, Ideals and Place in History* (New York: Harper, 1923), p. 75.
[4] A. Hyma, op. cit., pp. 54-58.

and so he began to explore various possibilities. The most famous one was located in the city of Deventer, where a semi-monastic order known as the Brethren of the Common Life had attracted considerable attention among both clergymen and laymen. During the second half of the fifteenth century about 600 books were published in Deventer, including nearly 100 classical books, whereas in other cities the figures were much smaller. For example, we shall list here some additional statistics in order to explain why Erasmus' father preferred Deventer to nearby cities. The first number indicates the total number of books published and the second figure indicates the number of classical books: Louvain (where the only university in the Low Countries was located): 251, 24; Antwerp: 350, 29; Utrecht: 51, 12; Gouda: 97, 1; Brussels: 41, 1; Bruges: 30, 1; England: 364, 29; Spain, with Portugal: 833, 41; Oxford: 14, 4; Salamanca: only five classical books.[1]

Moreover, there were in the city school of Deventer some very fine teachers, and the Brethren of the Common Life had their headquarters in Deventer. They had taken excellent care of a certain young man known later as Thomas à Kempis, who had issued in a new form the most famous book ever composed in Europe, entitled *The Imitation of Christ*. Gerard was obviously well aware of these developments and he persuaded his former housekeeper in or about the year 1475 to take his son with her to Deventer, where he remained from 1475 to 1479, and from 1481 to 1483.

In the year 1947 a valuable book was published in the city of Naarden in the Netherlands. It had a curious title: *Coster – Niet Gutenberg*. Its author was Jan Poorten. He presented on p. 33 a list of figures concerning the Dutch publishers during the fifteenth century, indicating that in Deventer 586 books were published, while for Zwolle the figure was 118, over against 51 for Utrecht, 5 for Nijmegen, 34 for Leiden, 20 for Haarlem, and 97 for Gouda. He mentioned the wonderful work done by the Brethren of the Common Life, which accounts for the excellent contribution in Zwolle. Moreover, they also had a school of their own at Gouda, which is reflected in the figure 97, as we saw, while the figure for Delft was only 29.

---

[1] A. Hyma, *The Christian Renaissance*. Second ed. (Hamden, Connecticut: Archon Books, 1965), p. 608. For a slight revision of the figures, see Kenneth A. Strand, *Essays on the Northern Renaissance* (Ann Arbor, 1968), pp. 62-63.

CHAPTER II

With the Brethren of the Common Life

We shall borrow here a few passages from the present writer's book on young Erasmus, starting with p. 81. On Erasmus' stay at Deventer the sources throw considerable light. Says Beatus Rhenanus, "His apprenticeship in letters was begun at Deventer, where he imbibed the rudiments of Latin and Greek... As a boy Erasmus knew the Comedies of Terence as familiarly as his own fingers, having a most tenacious memory and clear head... The ability of Erasmus was soon shown by the quickness with which he understood and the fidelity with which he retained whatever he was taught, surpassing all the other boys of his age."[1] These remarks seem to disprove the tradition according to which Erasmus was dull in his early school years.

Beatus Rhenanus should have known what he was talking about, for he was a close friend of Erasmus for a long time, as all the authorities on the Northern Renaissance well know. Moreover, he added some more pertinent remarks: "Among the Brothers of the Common Life was John Sintheim, a man of good learning for that time, as is shown by the Grammatical Commentaries which he published, and who attained a great name in the schools of Germany. This class of longcloaked cenobites are employed in the work of education; and Sintheim was so delighted with the progress of Erasmus that on one occasion he embraced the boy, exclaiming, 'Well done, Erasmus, the day will come when thou wilt reach the highest summit of erudition'; and having said this, dismissed him with a kiss."[2]

Erasmus stated in his autobiography, which we have mentioned above, that "this school was still barbarous. The *Pater Meus* was read over, and the boys had to say their tenses; *Ebrardus* and *Joannes de Garlandia* were read aloud. But Alexander Hegius and Zinthius were

---

[1] F. M. Nichols, *The Epistles of Erasmus* (reprint by Russell & Russell, New York, 1962), Vol. I, p. 23.
[2] F. M. Nichols, *op. cit.*, p. 25.

beginning to introduce some better literature; and at last from his other playmates who were in Zinthius' class, he got scent of the better learning ... In this school he reached the third class."¹ The *Pater Meus* was a series of declensions, and the *Tempora*, or *Tenses*, a collection of conjugations. Moreover, the metrical grammar of Ebrardus of Bethune in Artois, who lived in the twelfth century, and the grammar of John Garland, who taught in Toulouse during the thirteenth century, were somewhat impractical and uninteresting. But when Alexander Hegius arrived in Deventer, the whole scene changed dramatically, as the present writer has shown in his book on young Erasmus and elsewhere.

At this point we must revert back to our reference to the enormous number of books published at Deventer since the coming of Hegius and his colleagues. Unfortunately, P. S. Allen and the admirers of A. Renaudet have obscured the actual situation in Deventer from 1483 to 1500. They have harped too much upon the lack of classical learning in Deventer and the imaginary pursuit of that same learning at Oxford from 1475 to 1500. Now let us look once more at the figures we have given above: Deventer, nearly 100 classical books over against 4 at Oxford. Furthermore, let us at the same time examine one of the latest productions issued in France: Charles Béné, *Erasme et Saint Augustin ou Influence de Saint Augustin sur l'Humanisme d'Erasme*. It was published in 1969 by the famous firm of Droz in Geneva. Here we read on p. 104 that Erasmus spent eight months at Oxford, that is, from June 1499 to February 1500. Béné was still copying the old legend issued by Renaudet, which the present writer has discussed on pp. 343-345 in the second edition of his book on young Erasmus. Instead of eight months it actually was six weeks!

Even more shocking is Béné's discussion of the attempt made presumably by Colet to have Erasmus as early as 1499 become a teacher in his school attached to St. Paul's Cathedral in London, whereas this school was not in operation until the year 1508, as shown in an excellent book on Erasmus at Cambridge published in the year 1963.² All of this shows

¹ *Ibidem*, Vol. 1, p. 7.
² Charles Béné, *Érasme et Saint Augustin*, p. 113: "On a pu se demander, avec JB. Pineau, si Erasme était sincère dans la lettre qu'il écrivait à Colet en octobre 1499. Malgré l'insistance de Colet, nous l'avons noté, Erasme n'accepte pas d'entreprendre, à l'Ecole de Saint-Paul, l'explication de Moïse ou d'Isaïe. Il se juge inférieur à cette tache." The book dealing with Erasmus at Cambridge is known as D. F. S. Thomson and Porter, *Erasmus and Cambridge* (Toronto, 1963). On p. 8 we read this: "It would be nearer the mark to describe Erasmus as a London Reformer." Professor R. H. Bainton in his book, *Erasmus of Christendom* (New York, 1969), says on p. 103 that Erasmus spent

that many scholars in both France and England still continue to exaggerate the influence exerted by the professors at Oxford during the six weeks that Erasmus lived there in the academic year 1499-1500. We must say with D. F. S. Thomson and H. C. Porter, the authors of the excellent book, *Erasmus and Cambridge*, that Erasmus should not be considered as one of the Oxford Reformers but as one of the London Reformers. And we would suggest that the book by Margaret Mann Phillips on Erasmus and the Northern Renaissance should be thoroughly revised. She was badly mistaken in alleging that Erasmus and his English friends in the year 1499 were more deeply interested in Italian humanism than were the outstanding professors in Paris and Louvain. Unfortunately many American scholars in recent times have failed to note what has been going on in Belgium and the Netherlands during the past thirty years.

Another false interpretation made in recent years by numerous influential scholars in both Europe and America is that concerning the work done by the Brethren of the Common Life at Deventer from 1374 to 1398. These writers must have been totally unaware of the efforts made by Gerard Groote and Gerard Zerbolt of Zutphen during that time. The present writer was the first person to publish three books by Zerbolt which indicated his profound learning. One was that dealing with the use of the vernacular languages by those who wanted to elevate the scholarship among the common people. The latter could not understand the larger part of the services in their churches, as is well known to the experts today. Furthermore, Zerbolt and Groote were deeply concerned about the attitude of those clergymen who reasoned incorrectly that the masses of the people had no right to read the Bible in their own languages. For that reason only one copy of Zerbolt's learned work on the subject has survived.

Since the relation between Erasmus and the Brethren of the Common Life has been misrepresented by the admirers of Professor Johan Huizinga and many experts in Germany and Switzerland, we must now turn our attention to the great services rendered by Groote and Zerbolt. Let us note carefully what the present writer said in his article published in 1947 as a part of the *Festschrift* issued in honor of Professor Leon van der Essen at Louvain, and reprinted in the second edition of his book on

five years at Cambridge, whereas he lived in London from 1509 to 1511. Bainton also says that "from December 1508 tot April 1511 we have not a single letter from his pen." Bainton overlooked the letter composed by Erasmus naar London on June 9, 1510. We shall discuss this letter in some detail below.

young Erasmus (p. 339): "As one example we may well give the treatment of Huizinga, which because of its excellent reputation may be considered a model. He paid practically no attention to the Devotio Moderna, saying that one could well expect from its adherants such neurotic attachments as Erasmus felt for his friend Servatius... Huizinga can find only half a page for the episode in 's-Hertogenbosch, out of a total of 274 pages. There he says that Erasmus and his brother were subjected to bodily blows, reprimands, and severity, in order to make them fit for the monastery."

We must also pay some attention to the book published for Professor R. R. Post at the Roman Catholic University in Nijmegen by Brill in Leiden (1968). Its title is *The Modern Devotion*. In the year 1952 he stated in the introduction of the present writer's article on *The Imitation of Christ* in *Archief voor de Geschiedenis van het Aartsbisdom Utrecht* as issued by His Eminence Johannes Cardinal de Jong, that Gerard Zerbolt was not the author of the three works published for the first time by the present writer. But in his last book he retracted his error, no doubt as the result of admonitions by certain officials in the Roman Catholic hierarchy.

Post went so far as to state that Thomas à Kempis was sent to study at Deventer entirely because its local school was his only attraction, rather than the Devotio Moderna. He also erred in saying that the writer was teaching at the University of Grand Rapids, Mich., where his doctoral candidate, William Spoelhof, sent him a copy of his dissertation. On the contrary, it was dispatched to His Eminence Johannes Cardinal de Jong, who informed us that a certain official had misplaced the manuscript, for which reason he was unable to return it to us. And President William Spoelhof of Calvin College later on was astonished to learn that Post had devoted 30 pages to his thesis, and yet he had failed to understand the best part of it. Unfortunately he used two different first names for Gerard Zerbolt, that is Gerard as well as Gerald.[1]

The present writer had published the three learned works by Zerbolt in the two leading periodicals dealing with church history in the Netherlands, and his views were strongly supported by J. van Rooy, the principal of the Geert Groote School in Deventer. The latter published his doctoral dissertation on Zerbolt. In the year 1947 the writer visited him in his school, where Groote and Zerbolt were obviously honored

---

[1] See Post's book, pp. 17-49, 328, and 521.

in suitable style. His Eminence, Johannes Cardinal de Jong, in Volume II of his famous work covering the history of the Christian Church stated that Zerbolt defended in his learned treatise entitled, *Super Modo Vivendi*, the institution founded by the Brethren of the Common Life.[1] The cardinal himself published one of the three works by Zerbolt as issued by the writer. It filled 100 pages. The others appeared in *Nederlandsch Archief voor Kerkgeschiedenis*, sponsored chiefly by Professor A. Eekhof at Leiden and J. Lindeboom in Groningen.

In the year 1965 the present writer published the second edition of his first book, *The Christian Renaissance* (Archon Books). There he indicated that according to Zerbolt, the librarian at Deventer, while Thomas à Kempis studied there, "the perfect way of life was to imitate the apostles in the Primitive Church."[2] Moreover, the constitution composed largely under his direction stated that the house was founded in imitation of the Primitive Church. And in verse 34 of Chapter XX in the *Imitation* as originally written by Zerbolt we read this: "See Jesus within yourself and view in Him all things, for He is the creator of all things." Zerbolt stated in his defense of the brotherhood that "every act of Christ is an instruction for us, as St. Augustine says." And at the end of Chapter I in Book I of the *Imitation* as issued first by Zerbolt he said this: "Endeavor therefore to withdraw your heart from the love of visible things, . . . and thus you will imitate Christ, for every act of His is an instruction for us."[3]

Now the question arises as to what Erasmus learned from the Brethren of the Common Life, first in Deventer and later in 's-Hertogenbosch. He said himself, as we saw, that he reached the third class of the famous school in Deventer. There were probably eight regular grades and one preparatory grade in the school named after St. Lebwin, as indicated by the present writer on p. 84 of his book on young Erasmus. The latter must have passed seven grades in six years. Godfried Toorn, who was the rector of the brethren-house from 1410 to 1450, had been a teacher in the local school. Erasmus himself mentioned Sinthius, who was his teacher and also a member of the brotherhood. At first the brethren had

---

[1] J. de Jong, *Handboek der Kerkgeschiedenis* (Utrecht, Antwerp, Brussels, and Louvain, 1947), Vol. II, p. 434: "De instelling der Broeders om in gemeenschap zonder kloostergeloften te leven verdedigde hij in *Super modo vivendi devotorum hominum simul commorantium*." Strange to say perhaps, we read on the title-page that Professor R. R. Post had carefully revised and corrected this fourth edition. But that had happened in 1947.
[2] See p. 573.
[3] A. Hyma, *The Christian Renaissance*, 1965 ed., p. 560.

depended for a living to a great extent on the copying of books, but the invention of printing soon forced them to find other means of making a living. For that reason some of them became teachers.

Erasmus spent one or two years in the city of Utrecht, to which episode the present writer devoted a chapter in his book on young Erasmus. There he acted as chorister in the cathedral. The writer says on p. 74 of his book that the parents of Erasmus could have found "no better guide than James Obrecht," for his fame as a musician was simply enormous. Beatus Rhenanus said that Erasmus was a chorister there, "where after the fashion of such churches he had been employed for the sake of his small, high-pitched voice." He may have remained here for two years at the most. Apparently he failed to make much of an impression upon the great musician we have just mentioned. And so we are not surprised about his refusal later on to refer to his residence in Utrecht.

When a serious plague ravaged the city of Deventer in the year 1483, Erasmus and his brother Peter returned to Gouda, where their parents died soon after their unhappy arrival. The latter had appointed some guardians, including Peter Winckel. The guardians advised them to go to 's-Hertogenbosch, where the Brethren of the Common Life conducted a school, as they were also doing in Gouda, Groningen, Liège, and Brussels. Even in Utrecht they operated one, which according to Professor R. R. Post finally became so efficient that it gained control of all the higher grades in the whole city, which also occurred in Liège, Brussels, and Amersfoort. But Post has taken some pains in his last book to make the school of the Brethren in 's-Hertogenbosch appear very poor and wretched, just as Huizinga had done before him. He went so far as to assert that here the brethren "had done no academic studies. were not especially suited to teach at the city or chapter school." Around 1450 there was a house in the Schilderstraat, under the direction of the *fraters*. "There seems to be no real reason why this school could not have been within the house." Post continues as follows: "Since there was usually only one school in any city, that is the one big school for the teaching of the Latin, it was so understood by everybody."[1]

It was Post's aim to show his readers that the Brethren of the Common Life before 1480 were anti-intellectual. Consequently, he took great pains to make the Brethren in 's-Hertogenbosch appear incapable of giving instruction in Latin, which was being taught in the large city

[1] R. R. Post, *The Modern Devotion*, pp. 392-396.

school and the chapter school. But unfortunately for him Professer Julia Henkel composed an excellent dissertation dealing with the educational contributions of the Brethren. On pp. 179-186 she discussed the situation in the house at 's-Hertogenbosch, which even founded a house in Nijmegen, while in the year 1475 it also set up school there. On p. 179 she makes this observation: "The school at 's-Hertogenbosch was instrumental in popularizing the study of Latin. At one time there were 1200 pupils in the school." Moreover, the present writer did a great deal of research in that city, and so he devoted a whole chapter to this house and school in his book on young Erasmus.[1]

In this chapter we find some material that contradicts the account by Post. Here we read this: "The school conducted by the brethren of 's-Hertogenbosch was named *de groote school*, or "the large school." It "seems to have been the only school of fairly large size in the city." The writer refers here to an excellent description by a Dutch scholar, whose work was carefully explored by the writer in person. Post also was contradicted by a capable Belgian writer, who sent a copy of his work on he Brethren in Belgium to him. Here this Belgian scholar severely reprimands Post for having misrepresented the work done in Brabant as well as in Liège and Antwerp.[2]

This Belgian scholar refers to several unfortunate errors by Professor Post in Nijmegen. On p. 20 he quotes the following statement made on

[1] A. Hyma, *The Youth of Erasmus*, pp. 128-142. Julia Henkel, *An Historical Study of the Educational Contributions of the Brethren of the Common Life* (University of Pittsburgh, 1962).
[2] E. Persoons, "De Broeders van het Gemene Leven in België", in *Ons Geestelijk Erf*, Vol. XLIII (1969), Section 1. This article contains 30 pages. The Latin summary on p. 22 reads as follows: "Innixus documentis archivalibus de septem quae olim fuerunt domibus Fratrum de Vita Communi, intra fines hodiernos Belgii, auctor addit informationes imo et correctiones quasdam circa quae R. Post congessit in suo opere: The Modern Devotion. Lugduni Batavorum (Leiden), 1968." The most important errors by Post are discussed as follows on p. 20: "Volgens Msgr. Post vervulden de Broeders drie taken: 'They copied and illuminated books. They preached and acted as spiritual directors to various individuals, but principally to two groups: the schoolboys and the Sisters. Thirdly they contributed in providing board and lodgings and even teaching and training for some schoolboys.' Over de eerste aktiviteit van de Broeders deelt hij helemaal niets mee, alhoewel dit toch belangrijk zou zijn om uit te maken of de Moderne Devoten door hun schrijfwerk geen voorlopers en voorbereiders waren van de Humanisten. Wat het lesgeven betreft, besluit hij 'Up to 1480 the Brothers certainly had no regard for study, nor for teaching at school ... There is no mention of any scholar or even of a teacher in their letters or in their lists of the dead.'" On p. 21 Persoons has this: "In tegenstelling met Msgr. Post menen we echter dat vanaf het begin de Broeders praktisch overal, behalve te Antwerpen schoolonderricht geven." This constitutes an extremely devastating condemnation.

p. 257 in the book by Post: "Up to 1480 the Brothers certainly had no regard for study, nor for teaching at school. . . . There is no mention of any scholar or even a teacher in their letters or in their lists of the dead." Persoons, however, informs us on p. 21 that, contrary to the sensational misrepresentation by Post, "from the beginning in nearly all places, except in Antwerp, the Brethren taught in schools." He also adds that in Belgium this work on their part led to lawsuits instituted by local teachers, as in Brussels, as well as in Geraardsbergen. He published an important document issued in 1465 by Philip, duke of Burgundy, Lotharingia (Lorraine), Brabant, and Limburg; and count of Flanders, Artois, Hainaut, Holland, Zeeland, and Namur for the protection of the teacher in the school attached to the church of St. Gudule in Brussels. He orders the rector and his colleagues in the House of Nazareth, where the Brethren were living, to stop teaching. Persoons is of the opinion that when the Brethren were thus forced to give up teaching, they started a printing press, publishing numerous books there. But when in the year 1491 they were placed in charge of the local high school, they quit publishing books. We might also ask other scholars who sided with Post at one time how Gerard Zerbolt, the librarian in the house at Deventer, was able to write six scholarly books, one of which (*Spiritual Ascensions*) exerted a tremendous influence upon Martin Luther.

CHAPTER III

At the Monastery of Steyn

Erasmus left 's-Hertogenbosch near the end of the year 1486, and then returned to Gouda, as the present writer has indicated in Chapter XIII of his book on young Erasmus. At first it seemed as if he would enter the Augustinian monastery of Sion near Delft, but before long he went to Steyn, near Gouda, which was a member of the Chapter of Sion. The latter ranked with Windesheim as equal partners in the Order of the Augustinian Canons Regular.[1] Several chapters in the constitution of Sion were identical with those in the constitution of Windesheim.

At Steyn Erasmus became a close friend of William Herman, who was the author of eighteen poems edited by Erasmus. One of them had the following superscription: "To the very accomplished and most learned gentleman, Peter Gerard of Rotterdam, Brother of Erasmus, On the Praise of Friendship." It was dedicated to the Bishop of Cambrai on November 7, 1496. The collection was printed in Paris during the year 1497, and the great humanist Gaguin supplied a letter of introduction. Peter had gone to Sion to live, while his brother hesitated during the winter of 1486-1487 before entering Steyn. It is difficult to tell what the reasons were which impelled both brothers to become monks. These reasons have been discussed by the writer in considerable detail.

The letters written by Erasmus from 1486 to 1493 indicate that he was not greatly displeased with monasticism. For that reason we must study with great care his comments about that institution in his notorious book entitled, *In Praise of Folly*, issued in 1511, and also his remarks from 1517 to 1521. Very interesting is the following statement addressed by Erasmus to William Herman: "What was there at Steyn so dear to me that it has not among these mischances been lost in oblivion? You

---

[1] A. Hyma, *The Youth of Erasmus*, p. 150.
[2] *Ibidem*, pp. 145-154.

yourself have seen me play the youngster, and have often laughed." He had studied under Alexander Hegius at Deventer, as is proved by the title of a poem in Ms. 1323 of the City Library in Gouda. This poem was published for the first time in the book by the present writer on young Erasmus, pp. 225-233. On p. 221 the writer has expressed an opinion which he now wishes to modify. Here it is: "Herman never ceased to admire Hegius, but Erasmus, as was explained above, after the year 1495 began to despise the man whose accomplishments from the standpoint of a true humanist were indeed very mediocre." Much will depend upon the definition of a true humanist, and we must not lose sight of the fact that Hegius possessed certain qualities that Erasmus must have admired.

During the academic year 1928-1929 the present writer took great pains to study the environment in which Erasmus during his first twenty years imbibed various sentiments and opinions. On pp. 204-205 of his book on young Erasmus he quoted the following statement by the famous humanist: "Wherefore, in order to relieve the memory of this burden, it will be better to intrust everything to the Holy spirit, that it may be present only when called and invoked as the situation demands .... If a book is to be written, let the Spirit fly to us .... We were wholly given to dry, weak, bloodless, and colorless forms of poetry, partly out of mental poverty, partly in blind imitation .... We wrote as boys, not for sensitive, but for Dutch, that is, very dull ears, and since we tried piously to suit their tastes, we pleased neither them, nor the educated."

The first section is drawn from *The Book Against the Barbarians*, while the remainder came from a letter to a friend who understood exactly what Erasmus had in mind during the period from 1495 to 1511. He stated in *The Praise of Folly* that the people in Brabant, where he had spent much time between 1492 and 1495, were extremely stupid. But in this native Holland the situation of course was even worse: "To these are nearly related, as well by affinity of customs as of neighborhood, my friends, the Hollanders. Mine, I may well call them, for they stick so close and lovingly to me that they are styled fools to a proverb."[1] Here Folly as a person ridicules the inhabitants of the County of Holland, where Erasmus spent the first six years of his life.

Erasmus thus admitted that in his youth he had at one time been so stupid as to accept the principles advocated by the Brethren of the Com-

---

[1] A. Hyma, *Erasmus and the Humanists* (New York, 1930), p. 65.

mon Life. When the latter told him at Deventer and 's-Hertogenbosch that it was wholesome to study St. Augustine and Jerome, he must have accepted their teaching. He knew very well that the brethren had always exhibited enormous respect for Jerome, and so had accepted him as their patron saint. Sometimes they had been called Jeromites, as Erasmus well knew. We are not surprised to read on pp. 201 and 202 of Vol. XII of *Studies in the Renaissance* (1966) that Johann Sturm, the famous educator at Strasbourg, was "sent by his father to the Collège Saint Jérome at Liège." The author states that "this school had been founded in 1495 by the Brothers of the Common Life." And so Sturm in 1538 "proposes a plan for a gymnasium, or school, strongly inspired by the memory, evoked with precision, of the Collège Jérome at Liège."[1]

Charles Béné argues as follows: "If we follow this analysis, Erasmus was at first interested in the Bible, the *Imitation*, the Church Fathers, that is, in Deventer and 's-Hertogenbosch. That he was encouraged to do this seems very creditable. But where can we find any documentary proof? Where are the documents?"[2] All that we can discover, so Béné continues, is that Erasmus must have been advised to read this material. But during the first years at Steyn we find no proof of Erasmus' interest in such works. On top of p. 20 Béné says that Pineau, Renaudet, and Hyma all agree on the assumption that Erasmus must have been strongly affected by the Brethren of the Common Life. "Renaudet adds to this that Colet and Vitrier then persuaded Erasmus in 1499, and 1500 to adopt heretical views. Our approach is different. We are interested in the attitude of Erasmus toward classical culture. It is at this point that we study the influence of St. Augustine." And so he emphasizes unfortunately the influence of John Colet, believing with Renaudet and many other Western scholars that it was Colet who for eight months strongly affected him at Oxford.

We are fortunate to have at our disposal a book divided into eleven chapters entitled, *On the Contempt of the World*, written by Erasmus about the year 1490. He stated in the catalog of his writing addressed to J. Botzheim in 1523 that he had composed this work when he was barely 20 years old, but in the preface of the earlier editions he put his age at 24 years. Many years later he added a most interesting preface, which the early editions do not contain. For that reason not all the printed editions have this preface, while the very important version published

---

[1] See the article by Pierre Mesnard entitled, "The Pedagogy of Johann Sturm (1507-1589) and its Evangelical Inspiration."
[2] Charles Béné, *Erasme et Saint Augustine* (1969), pp. 17-21.

in 1641 by John Maire at Leiden starts with the text itself. The preface declared that the treatise was addressed to a certain Jodocus, who was supposed to have been a nephew of the author. The edition issued by Erasmus himself has this superscription: "Theodore of Haarlem to his Nephew Jodocus." In the catalog of 1523 we note that he wrote the treatise for a friend who wanted to persuade his nephew to become a monk. About the year 1521 he added a twelfth chapter in which he severely condemned monasticism. This seemed the proper thing to do, since a rival of Erasmus had obtained a copy of the eleven chapters, and he intended to reveal that Erasmus around the year 1490 supported monasticism.[1]

Some outstanding scholars in recent years have come to the conclusion that Erasmus seldom if ever was subject to drastic changes in his mode of living and thinking. However, we can find drastic reversals in his habits. For example, one of these he reported himself in a letter addressed to a superior in the monastery of Steyn.[2] He said: "For if I gave way at one time to the emotions of youth, that has been corrected by age and experience." He also stated that "it was by the pertinacity of my guardians and the importunate exhortations of others, I was driven rather than persuaded to that kind of life." Professor P. S. Allen early in the year 1932 told the present writer in his home on the campus of Oxford University that he was very peeved at the writer's friend, Wouter Nijhoff, the famous publisher in The Hague, for having issued a German book devoted entirely to Erasmus' skeleton in Basel. The author intimated that Erasmus had suffered from a terrible venereal disease.

Much has been written about the book entitled, *On the Contempt of the World*. Moreover, in the year 1967 a reprint of the English version issued in 1533 was published by Scholars' Facsimiles & Reprints.[3] The editor has taken pains to indicate that in this learned work by Erasmus many references are made to Greek and Latin classics. It is not difficult to see that *De Contemptu Mundi* was actually a humanistic production rather than a work devoted to orthodox Christian principles. The scholastic writers receive extremely little attention, whereas pagan and immoral persons are regarded with unconcealed admiration. Such an attitude could have been expected of a young student who declared in 1497 that this professors at the University of Paris had "rotten" brains.

This same subject has been treated at some length by Professor

[1] A. Hyma, *The Youth of Erasmus*, pp. 167-175.
[2] A. Hyma, *Erasmus and the Humanists* (New York, 1930), pp. 15-17.
[3] The editor was William J. Hirten, and the place of publication, Gainesville, Florida.

Roland H. Bainton in his lecture delivered in January 1967 before the American Council of Learned Societies, and published by that august body in its *Newsletter* dated May 1968. In the course of his lecture, Bainton made a statement about another humanistic production by Erasmus entitled, *Book Against the Barbarians*, which we shall analyze soon. He had this to say: "Having discovered that the tract *Against the Barbarians* was in a measure reworked, Hyma assumed that the same was true of another tract of the monastic period which we have only in the printed version of 1521, though it was composed thirty-five years earlier, namely the tract *On the Contempt of the World.*" Bainton reasons that "the treatise in the first place was a literary exercise, belonging to the genre of declamations on a particular theme, pro and con . . . . I would suggest, in the absence of proof, that the twelfth chapter of *De Contemptu Mundi* is the outline of the dissuasive with regard to monasticism, and possibly written later, may perfectly well have been coincident with the final draft."

One viewpoint of the present writer that has been attacked by some European experts is that Erasmus in his first book paid very little attention to Biblical passages and teachings. Bainton refers to this development in his lecture delivered before the American Council of Learned Societies in the year 1967. There he mentions the adverse criticism by Ernst-Wilhelm Kohls expressed in his large work entitled, *Die Theologie des Erasmus*.[1] The first book by Erasmus is to be found in the famous *Opera* published at Leiden from 1703 tot 1706, and referred to as L. B. by numerous experts.[2] Here we are informed that the author called Theodore of Haarlem wrote this composition in order to persuade a relative named Jodocus to enter a monastery. Here the title of the treatise is not given as *De Contemptu Mundi*, but as *De Contemtu Mundi*. The learned editor must have used a manuscript in which Erasmus had presented a wrong spelling. First there is in the text a reference to David and Solomon, next to Ulysses and Homer. The reader is warned about a siren near Charybdium. Next comes a reference to Syrtium and Syrtes. After that we find a mention of the Scriptures (the Bible), where we read that many persons are broken by calamities. But no specific text is given. In Chapter II we note the name of Sapiens, which may refer to the apocryphal book known as *The Wisdom of Sapiens*, or *The Wisdom of Jesus The Son of Sirach*. This source says that he who loves

---

[1] See Vol. II (Basel, 1966), p. 36, note 45.
[2] See Vol. V, col. 1239-1240.

danger will fall into it. At the beginning of p. 2 there is a poem in which the name of Palinure appears.

Next we meet the names of Virgil, Ulysses, and Flaccus Horace, Eutrapelus, Horace, Tagus, Pactolus, Plato, Cicero, Cato, Pythagoras, Numinis, Segor, Sodom, St. Jerome, Juvenal, Alexander, Xerxes, Hannibal, Paulus Aemilius, Julius, Pompei, Alexander, the pyramids, Cicero, Horace, Tithonos, Nestores, Sibyllas, Mathusalemos, Agricola, Syllana, Croesus, Thuscis, Chremes, Babylon, Jerusalem, Lucan, Daedaleis, Hercules, Cicero, Terence, Hegius, Democritus, Juvenal, Elijah, Moses, Egypt, Sinai, Jordan, Joannes homine major, utpote Angelus Dei, Jesus, Christ, Pythagoras, Platonic Academy, Crates, Juvenal, Orestes, Lucius Sylla, St. Bernard, St. Bernard, Argivus, Jerome, Augustine, Ambrose, Cyprian, Lactantius, Thomas Aquinas, Albertus Magnus, and Christ.

On p. 95 of the English version issued in 1533 and 1967 there is an actual quotation from the Bible, namely, the famous message by Christ, who said: "Take my yoke upon you, for my yoke is easy and my burden is light." But His name is not given, nor is the reader informed just where the text is to be found. On p. 107 Terence is mentioned, and the name of Alexander Hegius appears. On p. 108 Democritus is discussed, on p. 109 a pharaoh, on p. 114 Elijah, on p. 115 Moses, on p. 117 Jesus Christ, on p. 118 Pythagoras, on p. 121 Crates the philosopher, on p. 128 Juvenal, on p. 130 Orestes, on p. 131 Lucius Silla, and on pp. 136, 138, and 142 Epicurus. The latter made a tremendous impression upon Erasmus, who, as we shall see in a later chapter, completely misrepresented epicureanism. We must conclude that our humanistic friend had a long way to go before he was ready to sponsor orthodox Christianity.

Unfortunately the attention paid by Erasmus to Christian theology has thus far been neglected by numerous writers. It was not until the year 1966 that a large book was devoted to his theology, which work we have briefly mentioned above: *Die Theologie des Erasmus*, announced by Professor Bainton on p. 3 of his intriguing lecture. No doubt Ernst-Wilhelm Kohls, the author, was strongly affected by arguments of P.S. Allen to the effect that Erasmus was born in the year 1466. He also did not realize the enormous errors committed by J. Huizinga, who likewise argued that Erasmus was born in 1466. For that reason the leading German and Swiss experts held their own symposiums in the year 1966. Many of them held the opinion to the effect that P. S. Allen had discovered the important version of the *Book Against the Barbarians* as found in the celebrated Gouda Ms. However, that discovery was made by the City Librarian at Gouda, who enabled the present writer to obtain a photostatic copy in the Royal Library at The Hague.

Kohls has tried to make Erasmus a much greater expert in the field of theology than he actually was, and his references to the first book by Erasmus on pp. 204-205 are hopelessly out of date. This strange composition by Erasmus cannot be taken seriously, as Bainton correctly intimated in his lecture we have just mentioned. The great humanist was merely exercizing his pen. Here Huizinga was right, which Kohls denied. The latter actually went so far as to accuse Schottenloher, Meissinger, and Pineau of having failed to note theology where they constantly are said to have harped upon humanistic labors on the part of Erasmus. And as for the present writer's discussions of the lack of Biblical references in the famous work known as *De Contemptu Mundi*, he has referred to the English version as reprinted in Gainesville, Florida during the year 1967.

Whereas Kohls mentioned eleven publications by the present writer dealing with Erasmus, an American scholar named John B. Payne in his recent book entitled, *Erasmus His Theology of the Sacraments*,[1] refers to three, of which one deals exclusively with the Sacrament of Matrimony. And in the latter section he fails to discuss adequately the writer's contribution, devoting only one sentence to it on p. 281. There he has this: "Cf. also A. Hyma, 'Erasmus and the Sacrament of Matrimony,' ARG, 48 (1957), p. 161, n. 42." Here we find a reference only to Mountjoy's reception of his wife two years after their marriage, which does not throw much light upon Erasmus' view on the Sacrament of Matrimony. This refers to note 42 in the lengthy article. He ignored Chapter XIV in *The Youth of Erasmus*, plus the writer's analysis of the views of Erasmus on the sacraments in general. Unfortunately his bibliography covers only four short pages. And as for the very important *Book Against the Barbarians*, he refers only to the antiquated treatments by R. Pfeiffer and P. Mestwerdt (p. 234).

We shall not in this connection discuss Erasmus' task as a reformer, for that subject has been reserved for another chapter. But we must take cognizance of his particular brand of religion, starting with the period when he resided in the monastery near Gouda. Strange though it may seem, already in the year 1488 or 1489 he wrote some remark-

---

[1] Published by John Knox Press, Richmond, Va., 1970. See the present writer's review in *Renaissance Quarterly*, Summer 1971.

able passages in his book on the contempt of the world, referring to Epicurus as being very close to orthodox Christianity. Ernst-Wilhelm Kohls, who wrote a two-volume history of Erasmus' theology, was the first important writer to observe his tendency to make Epicurus appear in a garb very different from that he actually wore, according to the Church Fathers. He stated that the Church Fathers hated "Epicurus above all other ancient philosophers, and in the Middle Ages similar views were held by the leading theologians, while the leaders in the Protestant Reformation also detested him immensely. The name of Epicurus was a nickname."[1]

Why then did Erasmus claim that Epicurus favored asceticism? He argued with Epicurus that the monk should be willing to bear a moderate amount of asceticism in order to avoid far greater sorrows and punishments later on. For the convenience of the average American scholar we shall quote a few passages from the English translation published in 1533: "For so that we shulde expelle and put away from us those fylthye and foule lustes of the bodye, that they lette us not to opteyne the swete and most excellent pleasures of the soule . . . . Fyrst as Epicure saythe, whose authorite I wyll not yet forgo to wante the horryble vexation and grudge of an uneisie conscience, is the greatest pleasure that can be." What he means is that one must get rid of the horrible burden of uneasy conscience by shunning evil thoughts and deeds. Here follows another piece of advice: "Epicure denyeth those thynges to be pleasures, the whiche because of greatter grefes."[2] And just why Erasmus between 1486 and 1490 chose to quote Epicurus rather than certain Christian guides is a puzzle. Nearly all the best authorities among the Brethren of the Common Life as well as among the scholastic leaders in Louvain and Paris would have advised him to refer to the Church Fathers or the medieval saints. At any rate, we must note carefully the title of Chapter XI in his first book: "Of the Pleasure that is the Solitary Life." He used the word pleasure in a sense that he would many years later incorporate in the colloquy entitled, "The Epicurean." Already in 1488 he was thinking about the value of mental and physical

---

[1] Ernst-Wilhelm Kohls, *Die Theologie des Erasmus* (Basel, 1966), Vol. I, p. 25: "Ist die Bezeichnung 'Epikureer' ein Schimpfwort. Nicht umsonst läszt Erasmus den Adressaten in der Epistola einwerfend fragen: 'In den Klostern Lust?'" Erasmus said that Epicurus advised "solche Lustgefühle zu meiden, die nachträglich nur gröszere Beschwerden bereiten."

[2] Erasmus, *De Contemptu Mundi*, English translation of 1533, ed. by W. J. Hirten (1967), pp. 137-141.

discipline required of all Christians. What every person needed above all other things was virtue and abstinence from all evil thoughts and deeds, in order to obtain spiritual power. Doctrines as such had little value, while discipline would work wonders for everybody. And so he contrived to build up a system of spiritual exercises.

CHAPTER IV

The Book Against the Barbarians

Erasmus' next composition was a purely humanistic production entitled, *Book Against the Barbarians*. It was written while the author served as the secretary to the Bishop of Cambrai and was able to spend his leisure time in the ancient Duchy of Brabant. Although this happened about the year 1492, the treatise was not published until 1520. Nevertheless we are fortunate to have in the City Library at Gouda a manuscript version of this work, which is dated 1519. There is a vast difference between the two copies. In the first draft we note no opposition to monasticism, while in the published version Erasmus presents some bitter attacks on the leading monastic orders, except his own, the Augustinian Canons Regular. Even so, he still has little to say about scholasticism in either version.

However, soon after Erasmus became a student at the University of Paris he grew very hostile to scholasticism and monasticism. His attitude remained very much the same for many years to come. As we shall see, it was not until 1532 that he returned to the principles which he had expressed in some sections of his book entitled, *On the Contempt of the World*. By the year 1492 he had become very disappointed with life at Steyn, and as soon as an opportunity presented itself, he escaped and accepted an offer from Henry of Bergen, Bishop of Cambrai, to become his secretary. William Herman of Gouda wrote him as follows: "The trouble you have escaped no one knows better than I, who am even now tossed about in the same storms. I often congratulate you, and think how happy you are to have swum out of the billows."[1]

The new book was begun, according to the preface in the printed editions, when Erasmus was twenty years old, or about the year 1489. It was completed in the village of Halsteren, where Bishop Henry had a summer residence, located about 20 miles north of Antwerp. It was

[1] A. Hyma, *The Youth of Erasmus*, pp. 182-183.

to have consisted of two parts, but the second section was not written, or at any rate, it never was published. The date of completion was 1494, and in the next year the author submitted his manuscript to Robert Gaguin, the celebrated Parisian humanist. But the latter advised him not to publish it, since in his opinion it would offend many powerful dignitaries in both State and Church, not to mention also the leading professors in the University of Paris. Erasmus enlarged it somewhat when he was staying in Bologna during the academic year 1506-1507. It was finally published in 1520, accompanied with a letter to Sapidus.[1] There the author explained at great length what Christianity really was, as shown by the present writer in the second edition (1968) of his book entitled, *The Youth of Erasmus*. In the original version Erasmus still adhered to the simple precepts of his teachers at Deventer and 's-Hertogenbosch, while in the printed edition of 1520 he added some bitter attacks on those whom he had accused of being afraid of the top monastic authorities. In both versions he expressed great admiration for the leaders in the early Christian Church. The latter, so he argued, was the outcome of true religious ardor, combined with sane living. In that church real miracles of healing were performed. There the Holy Spirit had enabled the Christians to perform all sorts of miracles. So there we find then dynamic Christianity at work.

A terrible loss of spiritual power occurred during the period after our first century. Gradually the church leaders gave up their task of imitating Jesus Christ. The latter had said that those who followed Him would share with Him vast psychic and spiritual resources. He said: "He that believes in me shall do the works that I do, and greater works shall he do, for I go to the Father." He would send the Comforter, the Holy Spirit, who would show them how to restore the glorious possessions that had been originally given to Adam and Eve. For example Irenaeus about the year 175 said: "Wherefore, His true disciples receiving grace from Him, perform cures in His name for the benefit of other men, according as each has received the gift. Others banish demons surely and truly, and frequently those who are delivered from such become believers and are in the Church. Others have knowledge of the future, visions, and prophetic sayings. Others heal the sick by the laying on of hands, and restore them to health. And, as we have said, the dead have been raised and have remained with us many years." (See especially Book II, Chapter 32, paragraph 4 of his *Treatise Against*

[1] *Ibidem*, p. 184.

the Heresies.) In the edition by the Society for Promoting Christian Knowledge there is a note following Book II, Chapter 31, par. 2. Here we read this: "This passage, by anticipation, contains a warning against Spiritualism and the attempt to set up communication with the other world by its votaries. . . . What shall we say then of those who do give sight to the blind, who do give hearing to the deaf, and who do cast out evil spirits? We shall and must say exactly what the early Christians said, namely, that they are the perfect imitators of the Christ, the only savior."

After the year 1529 he was well aware of the fact that blessed are those who know how to control their physical appetites. He had often suffered from indigestion, and no doubt he discovered soon enough that gluttony in eating and drinking was folly pure and simple. And as for the third form of gluttony, he could hardly escape the thought that a person who preserves a highly potent fluid rather than squanders it on a fleeting form of physical pleasure will in the end be well ahead of his stupid neighbor.

Perhaps the most important problem for Erasmus was to find a proper balance between classical antiquity and primitive Christianity. In his illuminating work entitled, *De Contemptu Mundi* he was struggling with a serious difficulty. How could he reconcile humanism with mysticism? First of all it would be well if we carefully defined the term "humanism." The present writer has devoted a new section in the second edition of his book entitled, *The Christian Renaissance* to this problem. On p. 594 he quoted a strange conclusion presented in one of the lectures published by the University of Toronto Press delivered in the year 1939. There on p. 68 we read this: "The classical humanism of the Renaissance was fundamentally medieval and fundamentally Christian." The following remark by Erasmus is quoted: "I can scarce forebear, when I read such things, but cry out: '*Sancte Socrates, ora pro nobis.*'" This is called Christian humanism: "Nothing in Renaissance writing is closer to the heart of Christian humanism."

Just what then is humanism, and next, is there such a thing as Christian humanism? We might also ask what humanist theology was, for this term is now frequently used by both historians and theologians. Humanism is really the glorification of things human over against things divine. But theology, as the word implies, deals with divine things and attributes. The typical humanist exalted human nature, while the typical theologian was engrossed in aspects belonging to God. The ascetic scholars, unlike their humanistic opponents, often suppressed physical pleasure, assuming that the flesh is the ally of the devil. Christianity naturally glorifies Jesus Christ as the savior of mankind, and not as a guide in the field of human pleasure. We should always be careful in choosing our words as we delve into the history of the Italian Renaissance. It is well known that the typical humanists eagerly sought to gratify their physical senses rather than religious aspirations.

In the Preface to the *Book Against the Barbarians* Erasmus told his friend Sapidus as follows: "That there is a certain marvelous force and energy inherent in us, dear Sapidus, I gather from my own experience. In my childhood polite letters were wholly banished from our schools of learning. Not only was assistance from books and teachers lacking, but there was no reward for stimulating my ability. Moreover, the whole world tried to frighten me away from the study of polite letters and to push me in the other direction. In spite of this, a certain native impulse – it was not judgment, for I was too young to have any at that age – seized me and carried me off to the haunts of the Muses, just as if I had been inspired. I began to hate all those who I knew were insensible to the humanities; I fell in love with those who delighted in them. As for the men who had acquired a reputation in these pursuits, I looked up to them and venerated them as if they were divine."

So here we have an important confession by Erasmus, which has seldom been discussed by those who have written a great deal about the great Dutch humanist. The present writer himself has also ignored it to a great extent during the past forty years, much to his regret at the present time. Erasmus was worshiping Italian humanists like Lorenzo Valla without understanding just what their philosophy of life really was. For example, Erasmus did not fully enough realize that Valla's book entitled, *On Pleasure* represented a reprehensive sort of humanism. Let us then repeat here a passage from one of Valla's works reproduced on p. 42 of the writer's book on young Erasmus: "You clericals act from compulsion, we from free will. You keep the fear of God, we the love of God. You would never have taken the vows if it had not been out of fear of damnation. That is the reason why the worst people, who despair of finding another occupation, come to you. One may truly name monasteries asylums in which outcasts seek shelter, such as bankrupts, slaves, criminals, wretches – in short, all those who have nothing to lose and much to gain."

Erasmus imitated Valla in preparing his colloquy or dialogue. He said first of all that in his youth, when he was barely twenty years old, he sought a quiet place in Brabant in which to meditate. Presently his dear friend William Herman, whom we have mentioned above, arrived upon the scene. Next came James Batt, the secretary of Bergen-op-Zoom. He was followed by William Conrad, the mayor of the village, besides Jodocus, a physician. It should also be noted in this connection that Erasmus had just prepared an edition of Valla's *Elegances* for the press, which afterward was published without his permission.[1]

A lively conversation is recorded in the *Book Against the Barbarians*. The present writer in the year 1930 made the following remark: "It shows that Valla's campaign against scholasticism had attracted the attention of scholars north of the Rhine." At Steyn Erasmus had studied Valla with great enthusiasm, and no doubt it was Valla's comment about the horrible conditions in the monasteries which impelled the Dutch humanist to imitate his method. When he suddenly left Steyn without the permission of his superiors and never returned to stay, thus violating all rules set up by the higher authorities, he indicated clearly what his motives were. The present writer in his lecture at the Erasmus Symposium in Ithaca College on October 27, 1969, discussed in great detail what Erasmus thought of scholasticism up to the year 1532. He did the same to a lesser extent in his essay prepared for the celebration at the University of Louvain, November 17 to 20, 1969. Unfortunately the publication committee at Ithaca College cut out one-half of the material, while the editor later on published an essay by R. J. Schoeck, who was not even on the program, and dropped the lecture by the present writer, who had been the first speaker. Consequently, we read on p. 126 of *Renaissance Quarterly*, Spring issue of 1971 the following report: "THE ITHACA COLLEGE ERASMUS SYMPOSIUM has published the papers presented at its conference of October 27-29, 1969. The volume is entitled Erasmus of Rotterdam: A Quincentennial Symposium (Twayne Publishers, New York). The contributors are R. DeMolen (editor), J. C. Olin (Fordham), Lewis Spitz (Stanford), R. J. Schoeck (U of Toronto), and J. D. Tracy (U of Minnesota)." Strange though it may seem, the present writer delivered the first lecture in front of several hundred auditors, whereas Schoeck said nothing. In the age of Erasmus this reporting would have caused the average historian to regard such a performance on the part of an editor as repulsive as well as very stupid. Erasmus himself would have been deeply shocked.

One topic often overlooked by those who write about the history of education is the enormous difference between the two versions of *The*

---

[1] A. Hyma, *The Youth of Erasmus*, pp. 184-187.

Book Against the Barbarians. Both versions are to be found in the manuscript used by the present writer in the City Library at Gouda. He still has the photostatic copy in his own home. In the original version we find no condemnation of monasticism, and abuses in the Church are not yet enumerated. But in the later version, written about the year 1518, Erasmus says that the average abbot fears nothing more than that his monks should improve their discipline.

CHAPTER V

At the University of Paris

Erasmus was ordained a priest on April 25, 1492, and soon after that left the monastery of Steyn.[1] One might well ask at this point why he was willing to enter the duties of a priest when in his compositions he was now imitating the criticism by Lorenzo Valla of the higher clergy. The answer is not difficult to find when we note that he was now trying to act as the secretary of the Bishop of Cambrai, named Henry of Bergen, as we saw. He wanted to leave for Italy as soon as possible, and both he and his patron hoped that the latter would soon become a cardinal. In that case Erasmus would obviously meet many high dignitaries in Rome. We must also bear in mind that he was extremely ambitious in seeking for himself great honors through his association with "the vested interests." Unlike Lorenzo Valla and other Italian humanists, he was by no means "anti-clerical." But as soon as he saw that the bishop's dreams could not be realized, he took the next useful step in going to Paris and seeking high honors there. He may well have realized that the day would not be distant when France would take over from Italy the position of supreme power in matters of high politics and superb scholarship. The advance of the Ottoman Turks was now ruining Venice, and the great arteries of world trade were shifting from the Mediterranean to the Atlantic. And Antwerp was becoming the greatest port in the world. Why then burst into tears at the prospect of a good promotion in France or the Low Countries?

Erasmus was now being advised to seek a doctorate at the University of Paris. He arrived there in the year 1495, as P. S. Allen has shown. The first year he spent at the College of Montaigu, which was under the management of John Standonck, a pupil of the Brethren of the Common Life at Gouda. This fact should not be treated with indifference on the part of those biographers of Erasmus who would want to know what

---

[1] P. S. Allen, *Opus Ep. Des. Erasmi*, Vol. I, pp. 160, 588.

motivated him in his various enterprises. The latter was by no means well endowed with a capacity for hard work nor with good family connections. He simply had to adjust himself to the rigors of poverty and lack of powerful friends in Church and State, unlike Hugo Grotius, his famous compatriot.

But he was very fortunate in his close association with Robert Gaguin, who also had come from the Low Countries. He was the general of the Order of the Trinitarians, or Mathurins. Moreover, he also occupied a high post at the royal court. Particularly important was his position in the famous university, where he taught Canon Law and rhetoric. Erasmus soon showed Gaguin his book on the barbarians, which the capable professor believed to be too antagonistic to the clergy to advance the author's interests. He wrote as follows: "You have undertaken a dangerous and difficult war against those who do not cease to attack Polite Letters." He thought that Batt's speeches were too long, and he suggested that the author had better not publish this work.[1]

When in September 1495 the *History of the Franks* (*French*) by Gaguin was being published in Paris, Erasmus hurriedly penned a letter which, though printed at the end of the volume, served in a sense as an introduction, or dedication. It appeared at a suitable time for Erasmus. On fol. 135 the date is erroneously given as 1499, and so in the catalogue in the British Museum the present writer noted that the date shown was 1499, whereas it should have been 1495. A superior edition was published by Trechsel in Lyon (1497), which states on fol. 123 recto that the first edition was published in 1495.

In his autobiography he discussed his experiences at Montaigu. He said that he had to eat rotten eggs there, and drank out of polluted wells.[2] Less than a year after entering this dormitory he had to leave the place, being ill, and he then returned to Henry of Bergen. He soon recovered at Bergen-op-Zoom, and after that he went to the County of Holland, where he was going to "remain among his own."[3] But before long he changed his mind and returned to Paris. This event proves that he was not yet completely hostile to monasticism. But the monks at Steyn, seeing that he was becoming a real scholar, urged him to return to the University of Paris.[4] In January 1497 he penned an epistle in which he said that he had recently fallen ill, but had recovered,

---

[1] P. S. Allen, *Opus Ep. Des. Erasmis*, Vol. 1, p. 153.
[2] P. S. Allen, *Opus Ep. Des. Erasmi*, Vol. 1, p. 51, lines 103-105.
[3] *Ibidem*, lines 105-108.
[4] *Ibidem*, line 108: "Sed ipsis ultro horantibus rediit Lutetiam."

thanks to the power of St. Genevieve, and not to medical aid.[1] In the year 1532 he wrote a poem in honor of this saint, saying that she rather than the doctor had caused the recovery. P. S. Allen stated that the poem was composed in or about the year 1532, while the present writer in his lecture at the Erasmus Symposium in Rotterdam during the month of July 1936 argued that in 1532 he no longer believed in cures by saints.[2] However, in recent years the writer has discovered that Erasmus from 1532 to 1536 returned to the ideals of the Brethren of the Common Life and the Augustinian monks, as we shall see below. He may well have written it in 1497, or at least he must have made some sort of a report about his illness. By the year 1532 he probably had forgotten some of the details.

We are better informed about the attitude adopted by Erasmus in the year 1497 toward scholasticism. This was the topic which the present writer in the year 1969 discussed at considerable length in his lecture at the Erasmus Symposium at Ithaca College. He had also made a careful study of the strange contrast between two different editions of a most interesting work by Erasmus on the method of study. In the original version issued in the year 1497 Erasmus did not yet recommend the reading of the Church Fathers, whereas in the printed version issued in 1511 he presented an entirely different list. The title of his work was De Ratione Studii, or On the Method of Study. The writer publisshed the two versions side by side in his article issued in Vol. 25 of Nederlandsch Archief voor Kerkgeschiedenis (1932). Another article under the same title was printed in Bijdragen voor Vaderlandsche Geschiedenis en Oudheidkunde, Vol VII (1936). That was a trifle shorter and did not contain the essay by Erasmus on the method of study. It appeared in the series of articles which constituted the lectures delivered at the Erasmus Symposium in Rotterdam during the month of July 1936. In the writer's article published in the Archiv für Reformationsgeschichte entitled, "Erasmus and the Sacrament of Matrimony," and reproduced in the second edition of the book on young Erasmus, we find on p. 374 of the latter the following statement: "Suffice it to state that in 1497 the author did not recommend the reading of the great Church Fathers, as he did after 1511, but chiefly the pagan classics . . . . In the later editions he mentioned St. Augustine,

---

[1] Ibidem, No. 50, pp. 164-165, lines 3-7.
[2] Reprinted in the second ed. of The Youth of Erasmus, p. 348. His own letter was still available in 1532. At that time the completely reversed his position on monasticism, as shown by the present writer in the two essays written respectively for the Erasmus Symposiums at the University of Louvain and Ithaca College.

Ambrose, Origin, Chrysostom, Jerome, and Basil. In all the versions he ignored the scholastic theologians and philosophers. For the medieval monks he had very little respect."

It would be well for the German and Swiss theologians if they would consider what Erasmus wrote about his professors at the University of Paris in the year 1497. Here are his astonishing words: "I have made fun of some pseudo-theologians of our time, whose brains are rotten, their language barbarous, their intellects dull, their learning a bed of thorns, their manners rough, their life hypocritical, their talk full of venom, and their hearts as black as ink." These words were addressed to an English pupil named Thomas Grey, as the present writer has shown in his book on young Erasmus.[1] On the same page the writer added this report: "In 1497 the gay life led by Erasmus in 1497 caused some of his colleagues in the Netherlands to make inquiries. Gaguin, the famous historian, wrote William Herman that Erasmus was leading an irreproachable life. But during the next year the rumors became much more ominous, and this time Faustus Andrelinus was asked by Erasmus to inform his critics about recent events." Unfortunately Andrelinus or Andrelini was himself far from respectable, being the author of several salacious works. The present writer on pp. XIII-XV of the second edition of his book on young Erasmus has alluded to the neurotic behavior by Erasmus during the years 1497-1499. The Dutch humanist was then in no position to attack the Pope in Rome, and for several years after 1499 he was well aware of his perilous situation. Consequently, he would not be anxious then to offend Pope Julius II by issuing savage attacks against him, contrary to recent publications issued by a number of American and Dutch writers. In a subsequent chapter we shall discuss this matter in much greater detail.

Erasmus wrote some colloquies and treatises himself that throw much light upon the problem under discussion. The conversations composed in 1497 were published surreptitiously by Beatus Rhenanus in 1518, and the official editions of later dates do not indicate what had been done in the early period. For this reason it would be useless to consult the *Opera* published in Leiden from 1703 to 1706, and usually referred to as L.B., being the abbreviation of Lugdunum Batavorum, the Latin name for Leiden. Many theologians and even some famous historians have overlooked this unpleasant situation among indolent writers.

We are greatly indebted to Professor Craig R. Thompson for the

---

[1] A. Hyma, *The Youth of Erasmus* (1968 ed.), p. 374.

splendid work he did in publishing the earliest colloquies prepared by Erasmus in Paris as a part of the whole collection under the title of *The Colloquies of Erasmus* (University of Chicago Press, 1965). There he devoted a large section to the material first issued by Beatus Rhenanus in Basel. It is entitled, *Part Two: Formulae and Other Material* (pp. 555-620). It is followed by one other section under the title of *Appendices* (pp. 623-641). On p. 555 we note that "nearly all of pp. 578-602, as far as 'against this hunger,' was in the original edition." Consequently, we shall now study this important material.

Thompson says correctly on p. 556 that "many of the idioms and some of the names are borrowed from Terence. As late as Erasmus' day, and even by Erasmus himself . . . Terence was classed among prose writers. The comedies of Terence and letters of Cicero were commonly considered the supreme models of colloquial Latinity and therefore the best to imitate. As a matter of course they stand first in Erasmus' list." We have observed above that according to Beatus Rhenanus, Erasmus knew Terence by heart as a boy. Thompson also is correct in telling us that "the names of some speakers are those of Erasmus' pupils or acquaintances in Paris or former friends in Holland." But he should have added the name of Brabant, for, as we saw above, Erasmus spent a considerable amount of time in the Duchy of Brabant. Today there is still the large Dutch province of Noord-Brabant plus the Belgian province of Brabant. His great patron from 1492 to 1495 was Henry of Bergen, meaning Bergen-op-Zoom, as it is now called. The present writer had to do a large amount of research in Brabant when he was preparing his book on young Erasmus.

Significant is the following remark on p. 559: "Sapidus greets his Erasmus. Sapidus conveys his heartiest greetings to Beatus." No wonder that Beatus Rhenanus knew so much about Erasmus' studies in Deventer! And once more we we must give proper credit to the scholarly work done from 1480 to 1498 by the Brethren of the Common Life in Deventer. They even had a school of their own in that city from 1534 to 1538, but the jealous clergymen prevailed upon the provincial government of Overijssel to to let them have their local school back.[1] The present writer failed to pay proper attention to the tremendous work done by the Brethren after the year 1498 when he composed his first book during the period from 1919 to 1924. They were particularly successful in Germany, as well as in what is now Belgium.

[1] A. Hyma, *The Christian Renaissance*, 2nd. ed. (1965), p. 609.

41

At this point we must once more consult Thompson's remarks about the pupils and other friends which Erasmus had while he was a student at the University of Paris. On p. 556 Thompson says this: "Similarly some of the names in new material added in March, 1522, are those of acquaintances we can identify . . . The main speakers in the original edition, besides Erasmus, are Augustine Vicentius Caminadus and Christian Northoff. Christian was, without question, one of the boys for whom the first formulae were made." Thompson on pp. XXII-XXIII gives us valuable information about him and Caminadus. Here we note that perhaps not all of the material was written before 1499, for we find the name of Thomas More here, whom he may not have met until he arrived in England. As for Christian Northoff, he and his brother from Lübeck studied in Paris before 1499, and so we may conclude with Thompson that they received some instruction from Erasmus while he was studying at the University of Paris. And Caminadus also received some guidance from Erasmus in Paris. "Evidently Augustine Vincent saved, found, or procured a copy of the formulae, no doubt when he was living in the same house with Erasmus." On p. 582 Peter says that "many theologians never wake up from their dreams." This is exactly what Erasmus wrote to Thomas Grey in 1497.

We must also quote some material from the colloquy in which Erasmus referred to the College of Montaigue, where, as we saw, he spent his first year as a student at the University of Paris. We read as follows on p. 351 in Thompson's collection. (It was first published in the year 1526 in the colloquy named *A Fish Diet*, which was his longest colloquy): "That college then was ruled by Jean Standonck, a man whose intentions were beyond reproach but whom you would have found entirely lacking in judgment . . . Within a year he had succeeded in killing many very capable, gifted, promising students; and others whom I knew, he reduced to blindness, nervous breakdowns, or leprosy. Not a single student, in fact, was out of danger." Since Erasmus himself had spent one year in that dormitory and had to leave Paris when illness prevented him from studying there after that time, he must have drawn upon his sad memory when composing this notorious piece of literature. He was severely condemned by the Sorbonne for this sort of action, which amused Thompson. The present writer, on the other hand, has stated on several occasions (notably in his essay prepared for the symposium at Louvain University) that the Sorbonne was fully justified in its condemnation.

CHAPTER VI

The First Trip to England

We have on several occasions thus far alluded to a number of serious errors made by some French authors who imagined that Erasmus spent the whole winter of the academic year 1499-1500 on the campus of the university at Oxford. And we have also learned that both Margaret Mann Philips and Frederick Seebohm wrongly gave John Colet the credit for having induced Erasmus to study the works of great Italian humanists. We now have at our disposal, as we saw, a book by two British scholars who wrote a fascinating work entitled, *Erasmus and Cambridge*.[1] It started as follows: "In the autumn of 1499, when he was in his early thirties, Erasmus spent about two months in Oxford. He was there as a private person – a guest at St. Mary's, the college of the order of Augustinian canons, to which he belonged – being still a religious on leave from the monastery of Steyn, near Gouda; now over six years absent. There he met John Colet and attended some of the public and popular lectures on the letters of St. Paul – so very unlike the biblical exegesis, dependent upon scholastic 'glosses', which had irritated Erasmus in Paris."

Colet had gone from the city of London, where his father was a sheriff, to Oxford to study at the local university. First the took the arts course and next devoted himself to theological studies. From about 1492 to 1496 he took the grand tour of Italy and France, and soon after that began his lectures at Oxford. He made a tremendous impression upon Erasmus, as is well known in both France and Great Britain. Erasmus met Thomas More near London in the late summer of 1499, and "he was captivated."[2] More had been an undergraduate student at Oxford from 1492 to 1494, after having lived in the household of Archbishop Morton. Those writers who in recent years have refused to withdraw their support from Seebohm's book entitled, *The Oxford*

[1] Published in 1963 by the University of Toronto Press.
[2] D. F. S. Thomson and H. C. Porter, *Erasmus and Cambridge*, p. 4.

Reformers: Colet, Erasmus, and More (1867), will not be comforted in reading on p. 5 of the book on Erasmus and Cambridge that Seebohm soon repented of his errors and "withdrew from sale all the remaining copies of his own book and had them destroyed." This happened in the year 1868, only a short time after it had appeared in print. However, in 1869 he published a second edition in revised form, having corrected some of his errors.

Very much to the point is the remark made on p. 8 of the book on Erasmus and Cambridge: "It would be nearer the mark to describe Erasmus as a London Reformer." The next sentence is also very important: "His affection for England was almost wholly a loyalty to London." Erasmus referred to four wonderful friends, all of whom had studied at Oxford but only one of whom was still living there when Erasmus visited them in London. Only Colet was there then, and he would soon remove also to London. In the early summer of 1504 he became Dean of St. Paul's Cathedral in London. Now let us examine carefully the exact words used by Béné in his book on Erasmus and St. Augustine: "From that winter passed at the University of Oxford dates his complete and definitive rupture with not only the theological systems of the Middle Ages but also with the conventional ideal which he the year before had accepted, namely, that of Mombaer, Cornelius Gerard, Gaguin, Bosch, and Spagnuoli, plus the bad experience at Steyn." That was the antiquated opinion by A. Renaudet, which was rendered obsolete by the present writer's lecture delivered in July 1936 at the Erasmus Symposium in Rotterdam. We need not present the original French here.[1]

Now we present Béné's reaction, as supported by the Faculty of Letters and Human Sciences at the University of Paris in the year 1969: "It is an error on the part of Renaudet, and this error can be traced to a phrase in the same letter addressed to Jodocus Jonas: *Superstitioni et ceremoniis minime tribuebat*. As a matter of fact, this phrase does not agree with Colet, of which there is only a remark in line 245 plus following, but with Jean Vitrier, of which the description fills lines 13-245."[2] Béné then continues as follows: "Renaudet affirms that Colet

---

[1] Charles Béné, *Erasme et Saint Augustin*, p. 105.
[2] Charles Béné, *Erasme et Saint Augustin*, p. 106: "Il y a donc eu erreur de la part de Renaudet, et cette erreur peut avoir son origine dans une phrase de cette même lettre à Jodocus Jonas: on peut lire à la ligne 136: *Superstitioni et ceremoniis minime tribuebat*. En fait, cette phrase se rapporte, non pas à Colet, dont il sera question seulement à partir de la ligne 245, mais à Jean Vitrier, dont le portrait occupe les lignes 13 à 245."

caused Erasmus to turn against the conventional ideal, but Erasmus did not need to be turned away, for the influences of Cornelius Gerard, of Mombaer and the Windesheim officials in Paris had been sufficient to lead him back to the situation at Steyn, if that had been his desire."

Furthermore, we have also at our disposal a learned work by the famous Professor J. C. Margolin entitled, *Recherches Erasmiennes* (Geneva: Droz, 1969). On p. 67 we read this: "There are two interpretations of the term *Atque inter veteres nulli erat iniquior quam Augustino*, namely, that of Pineau and that of A. Hyma. The first, which is manifestly an attempt 'to save Erasmus,' reads like this: 'In his love for Augustine he was unfair to the other Fathers of the Church.' In reality, so thinks Hyma, and I shall depend upon his judgment, in 1521 he ruptured with Luther, the Augustinian monk, and it did not displease him in breaking somewhat with the truth to undermine the authority of Augustine."[1]

The book on Erasmus and Cambridge informs us on p. 9 that William Grocin in December 1499 was Vicar of St. Lawrence Jewry, near the Guildhall; Thomas Linacre was "practising as a doctor in the City; Thomas More was at Lincoln's Inn." Consequently, it no longer looks well to intimate that Erasmus in 1499 was dealing with the Oxford Reformers. It must seem strange that for many years now a majority of American theologians and historians have clung tenaciously to the term "Oxford Reformers," including the present writer himself. The latter in the year 1951 published an article in *Nederlandsch Archief voor Kerkgeschiedenis* entitled, "Erasmus and the Oxford Reformers, 1503-1519." Erasmus himself never taught at Oxford, but he operated as a professor at Cambridge University from 1511 to 1514. During his second trip to England in 1506 he spent much time in London, where he and More prepared their edition of 32 works by Lucian, and from 1509 to 1511 he lived for the most part in and near London. He composed the first part of his famous *Praise of Folly* in More's house in London.

We must now inspect the famous remark by A. Renaudet to the effect that "from that winter passed at the University of Oxford dates his complete and definitive rupture with not only the theological systems of the Middle Ages but also with the conventional ideal which he the year before still accepted under the influence of Mombaer, Cornelius Gerard, Gaguin, Bosch, and Spagnuoli." Mombaer was one of the most

---

[1] Here are the most important words: "Deux interprétations de l'adjectif *iniquior* ont été proposées, celle de Pineau et celle d' A. Hyma."

influential missionaries sent to France by the Windesheim Congregation. The present writer devoted pp. 236-275 in his book, *The Christian Renaissance*, to their work, including the labors spent by Standonck at Montaigu. He described in particular Standonck's dormitory. It is interesting to note that Standonck had been educated at Gouda by the Brethren of the Common Life, and obviously it was perfectly natural for Erasmus to spend his first year in Paris at Standonck's college.

In the year 1498 he wrote a sympathetic letter to John Mombaer. He encouraged the Dutch missionaries in France, and he told Mombaer that he had discussed their work with Standonck. After he had left Montaigu and returned to Steyn, he still could not forget his friends in Paris. And it does not seem likely that he would soon forget how kind his colleagues in and near Gouda were to him when he wished to return to Paris after his illness. We must also remember at this point that Erasmus was staying in Oxford in the house operated by members of his own order. That may well have escaped the attention of the famous Renaudet, who appeared at the Erasmus Symposium to represent France while the present writer was the official American speaker. Both men had some conversations in Rotterdam, and the writer enabled Renaudet to rent a certain suit from a local taylor. He discussed Renaudet's thesis at great length in his lecture entitled, "Erasmus and the Oxford Reformers." He was actually surprised that Béné had the courage to attack Renaudet's theory.

One of Erasmus' pupils in Paris was William Blount, Lord Mountjoy. He was living in a dormitory for English students in Paris, where he met among others Thomas Grey. It was to the latter that Erasmus in 1497 wrote the infamous letter we have discussed above. There he had said some mean things about leading scholastic professors in the local university. Renaudet and his admirers must have overlooked the statements made by Erasmus about Standonck and certain professors at the Sorbonne. And there can be no doubt in our minds that Erasmus made certain remarks to William Blount about his professors that John Colet would not have enjoyed. Moreover, when young Blount returned to England from Paris he took Erasmus along with him. It was he, therefore, who enabled Erasmus to meet the so-called Oxford Reformers.

Somewhat astonishing is a certain letter which Erasmus in the year 1499 wrote to his friend Faustus Andrelini, who had been a great ally of his. And when the Dutch monk had been reprimanded by his associates at Steyn for certain bad habits and neurotic attachments, he called upon Andrelini to defend him. This matter the present writer has discussed in the essay published in front of his second edition of the book on young Erasmus. Thus it happened that soon after Erasmus had arrived at Blount's home in England, he wrote a most interesting letter to Andrelini. He said this: "There are nymphs here with divine features, so gentle and kind that you may well prefer them to your Camenae.... Oh Faustus, if you had once tasted how sweet and fragant those kisses are, you would indeed wish to be a traveler, not for ten years, like Solon, but for your whole life in England."[1] He was referring to the kind deeds on the part of young husbands in England who prevailed upon their sweet wives to let them kiss their male friends. It begins to look very much as if Renaudet and Seebohm, plus many other writers, have been misled by certain facts which they selected to the exclusion of others in formulating erroneous ideas of their own not in keeping with the actual events. Blount's home in England is usually overlooked by these authors.

What we must do now is to investigate certain developments in the English boarding-house where Erasmus spent a considerable amount of time tutoring English students. It is very interesting to study the colloquies which Erasmus composed in that house. Thompson naturally was puzzled by the following names: George, Peter, Henry, Nicholas, and John. We are also wondering about the following conversation on p. 606: "Boy. Greetings, Erasmus; somebody at the door asks you to come out. Eras. Who is it? Boy. He says he's More's servant; that his master has arrived from Britain and wishes you to go and see him, since he leaves for Germany at dawn. Eras. Christian, let the bill be drawn up, for I must be off. Chris. I'll look after the bill for this dinner, most learned Erasmus." Thompson has assured us that this material appeared in the original edition. Consequently, the question arises as to the first meeting of Erasmus and Sir Thomas More, who is usually considered as one of the Oxford Reformers, although he was living in London during the year 1499.

We are also distressed by Erasmus' remarks about his brother Peter when he complained about the manner in which he was induced to enter the monastery at Steyn. Here are his awful words about Peter: "For him the affair turned out well; for he was a man of dull mind, but lusty body; selfish, cunning, and artful; a thief, a drunkard, and a voluptuary; in short, so different from his younger brother that one might imagine him to be a changeling. He was his brother's evil genius. Not long afterward he played the part among his companions that Iscariot played among the Apostles .... You have here the confession of a Judas; would

[1] A. Hyma, *The Youth of Erasmus* (1968 ed.), p. 377.

that he had followed his example and hanged himself before he had committed such an unfraternal deed!"[1]

Now let us ask ourselves what motivated Erasmus in leaving for England and where in England did he go first? The innocent reader might well guess that he went straight to Oxford. If such had been the case, who took him along? Can we imagine that he knew enough English at that time to go all alone to Oxford? On the contrary, his old friend Blount was his first companion and had him lodge in one of his sumptuous homes. There he met Thomas More one day. Moreover, Blount became the tutor of King Henry VIII before the latter inherited the throne from his father. Since three of the four so-called Oxford Reformers were living in London at that time and Erasmus was lodged in Blount's home, far from Oxford, poor Erasmus must have wondered how he was going to make himself the fifth member of that august assembly named the Oxford Reformers. The present writer during the period from 1932 to 1951 published three articles in two Dutch periodicals entitled, "Erasmus and the Oxford Reformers." He was stupid enough not to wonder what made Erasmus one of those Oxford Reformers.

Since these three articles are not readily accessible to the average American reader, we shall quote here a few lines from the reprint of one of them in the second edition of the book on young Erasmus: "In studying this biography of Colet by Erasmus, it must be borne in mind that the author had considerably altered his views on monasticism and religion in general. The scattered bits of information he presented to the literary world in 1521 were selected at will by the author of *The Praise of Folly*. 'I should add,' writes Erasmus in 1521, 'that, among the old authors, there was none to whom he was more unfavorable than Augustine.'"[2] This was simply a plain and deliberate falsehood composed at the time when he was swayed by motives far different from those which he sponsored in the year 1499. Professor J. C. Margolin in his superb work entitled, *Recherches Erasmienne*, which we have discussed above, states that in 1521 Erasmus was preoccupied with the operations of Professor Martin Luther at Wittenberg, his future opponent and he was most unfair to both Colet and St. Augustine.[3]

---

[1] A. Hyma, *The Youth of Erasmus*, pp. 146-147.   [2] A. Hyma, *The Youth of Erasmus*, p. 352.
[3] J. C. Margolin, *Recherches Erasmiennes* (Geneva, 1969), p. 67: "En réalité, pense Hyma – et je penche personnellement pour son interprétation – en 1521, époque où cette lettre-portrait a été écrit, Erasme est en rupture ouverte avec Luther, moine augustin, et il ne lui déplaît pas, même au prix de certains accommodements avec le vérité, de miner un peu l'autorité d' Augustin."

Colet and More, before they met Erasmus in 1499, were thoroughly medieval in their outlook upon religion. Both at one time seriously thought of entering a monastery, and they were both ascetic. Colet felt real reverence for the priesthood, and he strongly upheld the sacrament of penance. As for his theology, he said this about classical writings: "If we seek to feed on the wisdom of the heathens, which is devilish, not Christian, we lose the principle of our Lord . . . . Those books in which Christ is not found are but a table of devils." And in his constitution for the school he founded in 1508 as an adjunct to St. Paul's Cathedral in London, he said that the pupils should read good authors such as have "the very Roman eloquence joined with wisdom, especially Christian authors who wrote their wisdom with clean and chaste Latin." Since the present writer has discussed in great detail just what Colet's views on religion were, we shall not in this work repeat all the issues involved.

The writer in the year 1957 published an article in *Archiv für Reformationsgeschichte* dealing with Erasmus' views on the Sacrament of Matrimony. It was reprinted in the second edition of the book on young Erasmus. Here we read that William Blount, Lord Mountjoy, was very grateful to Erasmus for having issued an essay in favor of married life. The young and highly influential English nobleman had promised Erasmus, when the latter was his tutor in Latin in the English boarding-house we have mentioned above, that he would take the Dutch humanist along with him to his beautiful home in Hertfordshire. This county was located a short distance to the north of London and south of Cambridge. There the young chap must have been very happy and comfortable. Unfortunately we see on p. 378 of the book on young Erasmus that the latter was entertained "at Bedford". The name was, however, Bedwell. There he lived "with the family of Lord Mountjoy." And it was here or in another house owned by Mountjoy that he composed a poem "on the English nation under Henry VII."

Here came one day the alert Thomas More, who met Erasmus and took him to see the children of King Henry VII. This pleasant affair was mentioned by Erasmus in his poem on the English nation. Since Lord Mountjoy was the tutor of Henry VIII, the son of Henry VII, we can well understand why Erasmus was so fortunate as to meet such distinguished men in person. Erasmus also stated with pride that he had been royally entertained on other occasions, as he went on with great glee in the story published in 1523 in his famous work entitled, *Catalogue of Lucrubations*. Does it not look strange that so many historians thus far have completely distorted the manner in which Erasmus supposedly rushed from Paris to Oxford? Seebohm's book on the Oxford Reformers was so popular in Great Britain that it was finally incorporated in the Everyman's Library. Here we read how Erasmus was induced to go to England in order to learn Greek, in spite of the fact, now well known to us, that no Greek was taught in any English secondary school until Colet founded his school in the year 1509.[1] And on the university level little was done also.

Béné admits on p. 104 of his learned book that Renaudet was completely mistaken in thinking that Colet impelled Erasmus to turn against orthodox Christianity. He goes so far as to say that Renaudet "unfortunately pushed his theses to an extreme"[2] And on the next page he continues in the same vein, admitting that Renaudet, "being faithful to the analysis of Seebohm, whom he cites frequently, wishes to make Colet a supporter of the Reformation."[3]

---

[1] See D. F. S. Thomson and H. C. Porter, *Erasmus and Cambridge*, pp. 56-57. It might be argued, however, that Erasmus would not have to go to a secondary school in order to learn Greek in England. However, even at the University of Oxford extremely little Greek was known. Here follows another bit of information in the book on Erasmus and Cambridge: "Greek was, to speak, everything the Middle Ages was not. John Colet was not a Greek scholar, but in the statutes of his new school he stated that the pupils were to learn Latin and Greek."

[2] Charles Béné, *Erasme et Saint Augustin*, p. 104: "On ne peut malheureusement pas en dire autant des ouvrages d'A. Renaudet dont les thèses, poussées à l'extrême, nous paraissent imposer des mises au point importantes."

[3] *Ibidem*, p. 105: "L'analyse d'A. Renaudet a pour caractère essentiel, à notre avis de solliciter la pensée de Colet du coté de la Réforme." Nevertheless, it seems almost incomprehensible how a graduate student at the University of Paris during the year 1968 could have won the support of the faculty in which he obtained his doctorate when he was claiming that in 1499 Colet was already the Dean of St. Pauls's Cathedral in London and was in charge of a school ten years before he himself founded it. We have discovered references to the founding in 1508, 1509, and 1512. These dates are not wrong, for the process of founding took four years to complete.

CHAPTER VII

Life in Paris and the Low Countries

Preserved Smith in his admirable biography of Erasmus devoted the second chapter to "the revival of antiquity." The period covered here is that from 1500 to 1504, in which time Erasmus did much more than assist in the revival of antiquity. For example, his most famous book composed in that period was named *"Handbook of the Christian Knight."* He spent much energy on this task, repeating many of the ideas which he had previously expressed in various letters and treatises, especially his first colloquies. In the latter he had made numerous references to his friends in Paris and elsewhere. During the first five years of the sixteenth century he continued to reflect in his writings the atmosphere he encountered in northern France and the southern Netherlands. He confined himself to a limited area, unlike his activities before and after this period of five years.

First of all he merely returned to Paris, in order to continue his labors. Strange though it may seem, he had spent only six weeks in Oxford and merely six months altogether in England, whereas during his third trip to England he remained there five years, while in the academic year 1505-1506 he alotted a whole year, as we shall soon see. On his return to Paris in 1500 he compiled a famous work entitled, *Adagia*, or *The Adages*. It was published by Philip Kreuznach in Paris, and it contained only 818 classical selections over against 3,260 in the celebrated Aldine edition issued at Venice in 1508. Nevertheless, it was a wonderful beginning, making him very famous in a short time.[1]

Béné's third chapter is entitled, "Return to France (1500-1501)." And the next one is devoted to Erasmus' labors in Paris, Saint Omer, and Louvain. These two chapters are very valuable. The writer is intrigued by the work done on Cicero and the first edition of the

---

[1] Preserved Smith, *Erasmus A Study of His Life, Ideals and Place in History* (New York: Harper), p. 36.

Adages, or *Adagia*. It shows clearly that Erasmus had not changed much as the result of his residence at Oxford. Nevertheless, Erasmus was powerfully affected by his friends in England, especially Thomas More, as well as John Colet. The present writer agrees with an interesting opinion expressed by Robert P. Adams in his book entitled, *The Better Part of Valor More, Erasmus, Colet, and Vives, on Humanism, War, and Peace*, 1496-1535. He writes ably as follows: "My inference is that if Erasmus had absorbed from Colet new ideas on humanist socialist criticism, he had not yet learned how to use them."[1]

J. B. Pineau also doubted that Erasmus was sincere in telling Colet how eager he was in 1500 to give up his predilection for classical studies and take up almost exclusively Biblical exegesis and the literature of the Church Fathers. He stated that "the humanist did not cease to divert the theologian."[2] Soon after his return to Paris he spent an enormous amount of energy on the study of classical Greek: "He hellenized with some sort of fever."[3] What is meant here by Pineau is that he preferred Hellenistic Greek to New Testament Greek. Plato and Aristotle fascinated him tremendously.

The present writer has been greatly encouraged by the use of the term "London Reformers" rather than "Oxford Reformers" by Robert P. Adams.[4] This is all the more remarkable when we note that his book was published in the year 1962, whereas that on Erasmus and Cambridge, which suggested that henceforth it would be most suitable to use the term "London Reformers," was first issued in 1963. Before long Seebohm's book will need a second revision, and much more severe than the first one mentioned above. Moreover, it will become increasingly desirable to pay proper attention to operations in Lord Mountjoy's home near London, where More met Erasmus for the first or second time, as indicated above. We simply will have to reckon with the question as to how Erasmus traveled from Paris to Oxford by way of Bedwell and London.

In returning now to Erasmus' work on the *Adagia*, we observe that this became one of the most noteworthy among his numerous publications. Preserved Smith reported that it soon became a standard work

---

[1] Robert P. Adams, *op. cit.*, p. 28. The book was published in 1962 by the University of Washington Press in Seattle.
[2] Charles Béné, *op. cit.*, p. 113.
[3] *Ibidem*.
[4] R. P. Adams, *op. cit.*, pp. 30, 32.

"used and quoted by everyone with any pretensions of scholarship."[1] He went on to say that Luther quoted it thirteen times within one year. An English translation appeared in 1539, an Italian version in 1550, a German one in 1556, and a Dutch edition in 1561. After having seen the *Adages* through the press in Paris, he remained there until September 1500, subsequent to which time he spent three months in Orléans. His enthusiasm for classical Greek appears in the following passage quoted by Preserved Smith: "By lucky chance I got some Greek works, which I am stealthily transcribing night and day. . . . I am determined that it is better to learn Greek late than to be without knowledge . . . We have the purest fountains."[2]

In April 1501 followed the publication of *De Officiis* by Cicero. Needless to say, here we have another example of Erasmus' admiration for the classics of the ancient world, as pagan as one could find in France or the Low Countries. Just before moving to Tournehem in the Low Countries, he prepared this edition in Paris. In the Preface dedicated to James Voecht he stated that this work was "a book of gold," which one should always have on hand in order to be well informed. He called it an *enchiridion* or a *pugiunculus*, like a sword against vices, more efficacious than the weapons of Achilles or Aeneas. From this powerhouse alone flows forth a divine source of virtue which suffices for all of our spiritual needs. It will indeed render us immortal! This was a strange way in which to imitate John Colet and his friends in Oxford, and later in London.

In May 1501 he went from Paris to the Low Countries, paying a visit first of all to his old friends at the monastery of Steyn. Next he went to Haarlem and then to Dordrecht. At Haarlem he found William Herman, whom we have mentioned above. He then wandered to Brussels, where he conferred with the Bishop of Cambrai, while in Antwerp he discussed various problems with Voecht, whom we have also mentioned above. Finally he found a more suitable place for a longer residence, namely the Abbey of St. Bertin at St. Omer, where Anthony of Bergen, his former patron, was then living. Here he met in the Franciscan friary a distinguished scholar and religious leader named John Vitrier, who had issued some scathing condemnations of a number of practices and doctrines current in Tournay's cathedral. On October 2, 2, 1498, the Sorbonne had forced him to retract these adverse criticisms.

---

[1] P. Smith, *op. cit.*, p. 46.
[2] *Ibidem*.

But he had continued to flourish. Preserved Smith went so far as to conclude that he preferred Vitrier even to Colet. Partly as the result of Vitrier's inspiration he composed a religious treatise that was to become a major guide to certain persons who were in need of suitable help in the field of religion and morals. It was entitled, *Enchiridion*, or *Handbook of the Christian Knight*.

The first edition was published in the year 1503. In the introduction it was stated that this work had been completed in the monastery of St. Bertin. It reflected the great influence of Vitrier, as the present writer has indicated in the second edition of his book on young Erasmus.[1] Erasmus' purpose was to revitalize the whole church in imitation of the Apostolic Church. It was Vitrier who wanted all monastic orders simplified. Erasmus' opponents were the same as those "barbarians whom he had so ably attacked in his *Book Against the Barbarians*."[2] The *Manual* or *Handbook of the Christian Knight* was the first independent work issued thus far by Erasmus, according to the famous German scholar K. A. Meissinger.[3]

Erasmus was addressing a person who had been approached by zealous monks, begging him to enter their monastery. He hoped that this man would not give heed to them but bear in mind that monasticism was not religion itself but merely a mode of life, like many others. The author would refrain from advocating either the state of monasticism or the opposite. True Christians could be found everywhere. The man addressed should read the Bible every day and especially Paul. Erasmus had been planning to issue a comprehensive commentary on Paul's epistles. He had become estranged from those critics who said that religion does not require the knowledge of humanism. The Christian Church had been badly harmed by the Barbarians, whose ignorance was notorious. He was going to help all Christians to renovate their great institution and lead them back to a consuming love for the Bible in the original languages, meaning mostly Greek and Latin. Unlike Wessel Gansfort, his learned compatriot, he was not interested in cultivating the knowledge of the Hebrew language, which was unfortunate for him. Erasmus was now interrupting his scholarly work in order to help a Christian soldier pursue the true Christian way of life.

It is somewhat amusing to observe that in his eagerness to please Lord Mountjoy, who was greatly enjoying his married life, Erasmus re-

[1] A. Hyma, *The Youth of Erasmus* (1968), p. 380.
[2] *Ibidem*.
[3] A. Hyma, *op. cit.*, p. 379.

commended in his oration in favor of matrimony that the monks and nuns should receive permission to get married also. What he did not understand in the period from 1489 to 1499 was that the main purpose of monasticism was to rise above the level of married folk. Christ had said that there were three classes of eunuchs. The first class were born that way, the second were forced into it, while the third voluntarily refused to use the organs of reproduction for the derivation of physical pleasure. Such was the message of Matthew XIX. That is the reason why Erasmus in his first book stated that marriage was a refuge for the weak. But now he was writing for the benefit of an English nobleman who talked about taking him along to England. This member of the English nobility obviously did not want to be told that there is greater virtue in abstinence than in frequent marital indulgence.[1]

It is interesting to note that in the *Enchiridion* the author quoted 170 passages from St. Paul over against only 70 from Matthew, which gospel he greatly preferred above the other three. Moreover, there were also 70 quotations from classical writers, of which about two-thirds came from Plato's works. This goes to show that the learned author even in such a pro-Christian book refused to ignore the pagan classics. Plato was admired, and we must note in particular that his comments appeared in the most important sections of the book. Virgil and Horace were also highly favored, contrary to the advice to Erasmus by John Colet. But strange though it may seem, Terence and Ovid receive very little attention.[2]

In chapter VIII, which contained the rules of Christian life, Plato is quoted in both Rules V and VI. Those form with Rule IV "the heart of the book."[3] Erasmus gave greater authority to Plato than to the Church Fathers.[4] This must seem surprising to those historians who claimed that Erasmus followed Colet with the utmost respect. He actually went so far that he placed Plato above the Christian writers in explaining what he called Christianity. Consequently, Béné concludes as follows: "Erasmus lost sight of the Evangelical doctrine and we see the authority

---

[1] A. Hyma, *The Youth of Erasmus*, pp. 376-377.
[2] Charles Béné, *op. cit.*, p. 128.
[3] *Ibidem*, p. 128: "Nous rencontrons Platon dans les règles V et VI, qui forment avec règle IV, le coeur du livre."
[4] *Ibidem*, p. 128: "Si Platon représente, après les Saintes Lettres, mais bien avant les Pères de l'Eglise, la première autorité invoquée par Erasme au point de vue du nombre des emprunts, il faut noter aussi que le ton qu'emploie Erasme à son endroit lui donne un rang exceptionel.".

of Plato substituted for the Scriptures."[1] Here Béné supports the thesis of A. Renaudet to some extent, after having repudiated the main part of it, as we saw. Robert P. Adams writes as follows: "It my be true (as Hyma says) that Colet did not induce Erasmus to 'break' with scholasticism in which he had never been seriously interested."[2]

Significant also is the remark by Béné about the influence exerted by St. Augustine upon Erasmus. He concludes that the ignorance on the part of the leading authorities is "almost total."[3] Those scholars should have admitted that Erasmus quoted St. Augustine more often than any other Church Father. Béné has devoted a great deal of attention to the signal errors committed in particular by Seebohm. We might once more refer here to the mistake made by Erasmus when he reported that Colet's view was more unfavorable to St. Augustine than to any other Church Father. We noted above that Professor Margolin made much of this important point, and strongly supported the present writer's opinion on that important subject.

Our next subject is the residene of Erasmus in Louvain, where he spent about two years, beginning with the autumn of 1502. Here he found an environment in which his own native language was widely used. In the year 1500 John Standonck and Adrian of Utrecht (later known as Pope Adrian VI) bought a piece of property for the use of poor students, and the Brethren of the Common Life operated a flourishing house of their own. It must seem surprising that few of Erasmus' biographers thus far have paid much attention to his residence in Louvain, especially so because from 1517 to 1521 he was a professor in the local university. Moreover, Adrian and his associates offered him a position in the same university while he was a student there for two years. But he declined this position. On January 6, 1504, he delivered an address in honor of Philip the Handsome, the ruler of several duchies and counties in the Netherlands. It was given in the royal castle at Brussels, and the brilliant speaker was warmly applauded on this important occasion.

In the summer of the year 1504 Erasmus made one of the most important discoveries of his whole life. He mentioned it in a letter addressed to Christopher Fisher, to whom he wrote as follows: "Last summer in an old library I was hunting (it is not the hunting in a forest

---

[1] *Ibidem*, p. 130: "Il y a plus grave. A force d'admirer le philosophie de Platon, Erasme en arrive à perdre de vue la doctrine évangélique, et nous voyons l'autorité de Platon se substituer à celle de l'Ecriture."
[2] R. P. Adams, *op. cit.*, p. 28.
[3] Ch. Béné, *op. cit.*, p. 141.

that is the most agreeable) and found a truly extraordinary prey: the *Annotations on the New Testament* by Valla." He was referring to an unpublished major work by Lorenzo Valla, which had lain there in splendid isolation. The library was a part of the Premonstratensian Abbey of Parc or Park near Louvain. Valla had issued a daring attack upon the New Testament as it appeared in the Vulgate, and Erasmus was well aware of the fact that if he should support Valla in this field, he would incur the wrath of many officials in the Roman Catholic Church. Nevertheless, he chose to go ahead with his plan to issue an edition of his own. He labored on it for two years, and so in October 1506 he completed the Latin text of the New Testament based upon the work by Valla. Ten more years passed until he finally incorporated it in the second edition of the Greek New Testament (1519).[1]

We find an entirely different account in the book on Erasmus and Cambridge, which we have discussed above. Here we read that "the Valla notes on the New Testament greatly excited Erasmus, and he published them at the Paris press of Josse Bade in April 1505, just before his second visit to England." We are also informed here that in the prefatory letter addressed to Christopher Fisher, whom we have mentioned above, he discussed many points which later on he would take up in much greater detail. He asked Fisher what was wrong with Valla's action in taking the liberty to make some annotations on the New Testament after having compared several Greek copies. Some were very ancient, while others had been corrected in recent times. Was it not of the greatest importance to discover just what the earliest versions stated? At that time Erasmus did not yet know enough Greek to produce the best version, but later on he would certainly be in a position to establish the authentic text.[2]

The book goes on like this: "Therefore it is true to say (as you so often do, my learned Christopher) that those who venture to write on Scripture (and not only Scripture, but any ancient books at all) without a reasonable command of both languages and literatures in question, have neither modesty, nor intelligence. For when men like these strain their hardest in an endeavour to show themselves as learned as the best of scholars, it is precisely then, as you see, that they become objects of supreme derision to those who really know the languages." Here then we see the beginning of the most important task ever undertaken by

---

[1] Preserved Smith, *op. cit.*, pp. 161-162. Ch. Béné, *op. cit.*, pp. 195-197.
[2] D. F. S. Thomson and H. C. Porter, *Erasmus and Cambridge*, pp. 45-46.

Erasmus, namely, to establish the first authentic text of the New Testament in its most ancient form. And this would lead to translations in all modern languages of importance, thus greatly enhancing Erasmus' influence in the modern world.

CHAPTER VIII

The London Reformers

In April 1505 Erasmus appeared for the second time in England, and now he remained about twice as long as he did in the academic year 1499-1500. During this second visit he spent the greater part in London. Hitherto most scholars have assumed that he did not arrive in England until the end of 1505 or the beginning of 1506. Such was the case with W. E. Campbell, the author of a charming book entitled, *Erasmus, Tyndale and More* (London, 1949).[1] He quotes the following statement made by Erasmus: "No place in the world has given me so many friends as your City of London." The letter was addressed to John Colet, who in the year 1504 had become the Dean of St. Paul's Cathedral. And so Campbell reasons that in London "he found the most genuine enthusiasm for learning." He also mentions the significant fact that "he was the guest of Mountjoy for several months." It must seem astonishing that hitherto nearly all writers who have discussed the development of the Northern Renaissance have concentrated far too much attention upon Oxford and far too little on London and Cambridge.

Preserved Smith shows that Erasmus himself in his biography of Colet started it as follows "Colet was born in London of honorable and wealthy parents.[2] "And in another passage we find this remark, quoted by Smith also : "From his sacred labors at Oxford Colet was called to London by favor of King Henry VII to be dean of St. Paul's, that he might preside over the cathedral chapter of him whose writings he so much loved. This is a dignity of the first rank in England, even though others have larger emoluments. This excellent man, as though summoned to a labor rather than an honor, restored the relaxed discipline of the chapter and instituted the new custum of preaching every holy day in his church, besides delivering other sermons in the palace and elsewhere."[3]

---

[1] See p. 40 of this book issued by Eyre & Spottswoode.
[2] P. Smith, *op. cit.*, p. 94.   [3] P. Smith, *op. cit.*, p. 98.

In his homilies, so continued Erasmus, "he did not take the text at random but chose one line of argument to which he adhered for several consecutive discourses." For example, he would follow the Gospel of Matthew in this manner, or the Apostles' Creed, or the Lord's Prayer. He drew large audiences in this way, including many of the chief men of the city in general or of the royal court. He reduced the elaborate and expensive operations of the dean's staff at meals to a more frugal management. At the dinner table in the afternoon he would hold an informative discourse "which was such a delight to only good and learned men." After grace a boy would read aloud a chapter from the Epistles of Paul or the Proverbs of Solomon. From these he would select a suitable text, "the meaning of which he would inquire from both the learned and intelligent laymen", At the end of the meal he would deliver another discourse, "so that his guests departed refreshed in mind and body." The serving of each meal was regularly conducted with proper dignity and speed.

Erasmus reported that Colet sometimes took him out in the country for a ride "which he enjoyed more than anything else." Their companion was always a useful book, and their "words were only of Christ." Colet was extremely well-mannered, and so it seemed natural for him to abhor all sorts of "barbarism or solecism in speech." He strove for neatness and prudence in the management of all affairs in the cathedral chapter of St. Paul's. But he loathed extravagance. "He wore only dark clothes, though commonly the priests and theologians there wore purple." He inherited from his father a large fortune, most of which he used in the founding of a school attached to St. Paul's Cathedral. This school he "dedicated to the boy Jesus." There he employed two capable teachers, who received from him large salaries, in order that they might teach the pupils without charge. He divided them into four classes. "Above the chair of the preceptor sat the boy Jesus as though teaching. Him the whole class saluted on entering and leaving." Above was the face of the Father saying, "Hear ye Him." Erasmus boasted of the fact that this arrangement was made at his suggestion. Preserved Smith stated in a footnote that "for this school Erasmus wrote a Sermon on the Boy Jesus, which was soon translated into English and has been edited by J. H. Lupton in 1901."[1]

Colet traveled widely in France and Italy, and he devoted a vast amount of time to the study of the Church Fathers, Thomas Aquinas, Duns

---

[1] P. Smith, *op. cit.*, p. 99.

Scotus, and both Canon and Civil Law. At Oxford University he lectured without pay to large audiences on the Epistles of St. Paul. Erasmus continues as follows: "There I first met the man, for some god or other sent me there." He was about Erasmus' age, being thirty in 1499 and two or three years younger than Erasmus. Here then we find some valuable information about the time when Erasmus himself was born. Colet never worked for an ordinary doctor's degree, but he did accept an honorary one. He considered the Scotists utter fools, in which respect he supported the remarks made by Erasmus to Thomas Grey in the year 1497, as we saw above.

It is in Erasmus' biography of Colet that the notorious statement about St. Augustine quoted above appears. Preserved Smith in the year 1923 quoted it as follows: "Among the ancients he was more hostile to none than to Augustine." Smith indicated how Lupton tried to solve this thorny problem in 1887: "But I cannot find any good lexical authority for so translating 'iniquior.'" Smith adds this comment of his own: "The text is surprising, and is either corrupt or Erasmus's pen slipped and put in one too many negatives. But see Allen's note, IV, p. 515, line 273."[1] We have indicated above that the explanation by Professor J. C. Margolin published in the year 1969 is the best one available to us now. When Erasmus issued his strange remark in the year 1521, he was beginning to break with Luther, who supported St. Augustine with tremendous respect and affection. The breach between these two men became terrific, as the present writer indicated in his essay sent in the same year 1969 to the Erasmus Symposium at the University of Louvain. And the consequences of this breach were dreadful in both Europe and the United States of America, as shown by the present writer in several of his recent publications.

The significant thing about Erasmus' second trip to England was his residence in Lord Mountjoy's home, which lasted for several months. It was the latter who enabled the Dutch scholar to embark upon his first voyage, and now, six years later, Erasmus took further advantage of his friendship with that powerful English nobleman, who no doubt received excellent instruction from Erasmus in Paris. As soon as this valuable information has become more widely known among our most influential scholars, they will begin to drop the name of the Oxford Reformers. Robert P. Adams in his brilliant book on the London Reformers makes this illuminating observation: "During the London

[1] P. Smith, *op. cit.*, p. 94.

Reformers' efforts at revival of ancient culture and reform of medieval ways, efforts persistently to be obstructed by wars and their aftermath, parallelels with ancient Roman conditions were not far to seek. With mighty strokes St. Augustine gave his view of a grand cultural drama in which Rome, once the epitome of culture but neglectful of vital reforms, succumbed to degeneracy within until overwhelmed by wars from without." Adams continues in telling us that the early sixteenth century was a time of agonizing reappraisals, "in which Colet's part has been ably stated by his best biographer. Not alone as an educational pioneer is he memorable; as Dean of St. Paul's during these years he had a vital hand in an epochal transition of cultures."[1]

Erasmus and Thomas More in the year 1506 published a monumental book containing 32 treatises by the famous Lucian in Latin translation. It was issued in Paris by Badius Ascensius, a pupil of the Brethren of the Common Life at Ghent. In the year 1935 the present writer sold a beautiful copy in a contemporary binding to the University of Michigan. He published an article in *Nederlandsch Archief voor Kerkgeschiedenis* entitled, "Erasmus and the Oxford Reformers, 1503-1519." There he committed an error while saying that Craig R. Thompson, in writing his doctoral dissertation on this work and some other treatises by Lucian, bewailed the fact that he had been unable to locate a copy of this marvelous book by Erasmus and Thomas More, while there was that wonderful edition at the University of Michigan.[2] The writer unfortunately made a bad mistake in reporting that Thompson was a pupil of Preserved Smith. During the summer of 1939 he once more examined the dissertation by Thompson, and he was shocked to learn that Thompson in 1940 was an instructor at Cornell University in the English department rather than the history department. His dissertation was accepted at Princeton University rather than at Cornell, where Preserved Smith was operating at that time. The writer held Smith responsible for the oversight on the part of Thompson, whereas the error occurred at Princeton.

It may seem surprising that Erasmus and Thomas More became great admirers of the scoffer Lucian. But the present writer in his article just mentioned says that it is by no means surprising, for "Erasmus, unlike John Colet, was not deeply religious, and his love of theological studies, in spite of his comments addressed to Colet, was shallow. His *Adagia* of the year 1500, issued almost immediately upon his return from England,

[1] R. P. Adams, *op. cit.*, p. 32.
[2] A. Hyma, *op. cit.*, p. 77.

indicated clearly where the treasure of his heart was. Lucian appealed to him, for he was a Greek scholar of his own type, sarcastic, cynical, eager to expose abuses, and devoted to elegant literature as an end in itself. There is indeed a marked contrast between the classical spirit and a book like *The Imitation of Christ*. From 1503 to 1506 Thomas More agreed with Erasmus in his zeal for a knowledge of classical Greek and what the Brethren of the Common Life referred to as "wordly wisdom." Lucian was witty, not humble. He enjoyed the things of this world and did not hasten toward the kingdom of heaven. Martin Luther, on the other hand, said that his kingdom was not of this world, and he condemned Lucian as a dreaded atheist. Erasmus was the man of reason, the satirist, who in his famous work, *The Praise of Folly*, deliberately imitated Lucian, rather than some author recommended by John Colet. Is it any wonder that Erasmus refused to remain with Colet at Oxford during the year 1500? But Thomas More was very different from Colet. Up to June 1514, Erasmus translated 36 of Lucian's works. Of these 28, together with four by More, were pubished in 1506. Those four translated by More constituted his first published work.

Among the humanistic writings by Lucian was one entitled, *On Sacrifices*. In it he ridiculed the idea of atonement, such as that suffered by Christ in person. He made fun of all religions, as many of Erasmus' contemporaries well knew. But Erasmus and More did not seem to mind at this particular time the animosity of orthodox clergymen, strange though it may seem. The first piece in the volume was dedicated to Richard Foxe, the bishop of Winchester, and the next piece to the Bishop of Chartres. It is worth noting in this connection that this translation by More was more often printed than any of his other works, but only one section of it, that of *Menippus*, was ever published in England. However, we must admit here that his *Utopia* in recent times has had far more editions than his translations of treatises by Lucian. The English were not much given to the reading of literature admired by Thomas More, whose nonsense in *Utopia* they despised at first.

The edition of 1506 starts as follows: "Erasmus Luciani compluria Opusculi longe festivissima ab Erasmo Roterdamo et Thoma Moro interpretibus optimis in latinorum linguam traducto." The most important piece is entitled, *Tyrannicida seu pro tyranicida eiusdem declamatio*. It seems that here five pieces, rather than four, by More are listed. The dedication of the first piece reads as follows: "Ricardo Episcopo vvintoulensi." And then we get the date: "London Calendis Ianuariis

MDVI." We also have this dedication to the Bishop of Chartres: "D. Renato Ep carnuten." On fol. XXII recto we find a dedication to Ruthallo, the Secretary of the King. And on fol. XXVII verso to XXIX verso is the notorious piece called, "Tyrannicide." Then follows a letter to Ricardo, fol XXX recto. Next a declamation by Erasmus, on fol. XXX recto to fol. XLIII recto. At the bottom is a piece addressed to Paludano at Louvain. Then follows an interpretation by Erasmus of Lucian on fol. XLIII verso. Next we have this: "Cnemonis ac Damippi dialogus," fol. XLIX by Erasmus. Next: "Luciana dialogi breviores," fol. L recto. Then appears the "Menippus," translated by More.

Very significant is the dedication to William Cop on fol. LI recto. There is the title of "de Senectute." Cop was the physician to the German Nation in Paris, according to Preserved Smith.[1] He was a native of Basel, adds Smith. Important also is the dedication to Busleiden on fol. XLVIII recto. Busleiden's first name was Jerome. He left a large bequest for the founding of the College of the Three Languages in Louvain, according to Smith.[2] Erasmus took excellent care of this bequest, and we shall hereafter have to say more about Busleiden and his colleagues. The notorious dialogue on sacrifices was published on fol. LIIII recto. Here Lucian scoffed at the idea of Christian sacrifice. He was among the most popular writers discussed by the leaders in the Renaissance movement. Preserved Smith reports that "Thomas More, Pirckheimer, Mosellanus, Ottomar Luscinius, and Melanchthon all tried their hands at versions of his dialogues." And here follows an important report by Smith: "Nor did Christianity escape the notice of Lucian, who directed his jibes against 'the man who ascended into heaven,' and against Christian dogmas."[2]

Erasmus not only wrote a detailed biography of John Colet but also one of Thomas More, which in the year 1519 he sent to the famous Ulrich von Hutten. We shall follow the English translation published in the book by W. E. Campbell, to which we have referred above. Like Colet, he liked to be "dressed simply, and did not wear silk, or purple, or gold chains, except when it was not allowable to dispense with them." At first he did not enjoy court life, and "any intimacy with princes, having always a special hatred of tyranny and a great fancy for equality. He could not be tempted to Henry VIII's court without great trouble,

---

[1] P. Smith, *op. cit.*, pp. 36-37. He informs us here that it was Cop plus St. Genevieve, according to Erasmus, who cured him of his terrible fever in Paris which we have discussed above.

[2] *Ibidem*, pp. 193-194.

although nothing could be desired more courteous than this Prince."
When a young man he took "a great delight with Lucian." Indeed it was
Erasmus who suggested that he write the *Moria* (*Praise of Folly*)." He
studied Greek at an early age, and also philosophy, whereupon his father
suspended his allowance "and almost disowned him, because they withdrew him from the learning of the law schools." Then he suddenly
changed his mind and took up the study of law so fervently that "there
was no one more eagerly consulted by suitors." Consequently, he made
more money practicing law than any other attorney in England. He
devoted much careful study to the orthodox Church Fathers, and while
still fairly young delivered a lecture on *De Civitate* of St. Augustine. His
audience was very large, and "old men and priests were not ashamed to
take a lesson in divinity from a young layman." He was born in London
and in that city he acted for some years as an under-sheriff, or judge.
Since the court in which he served as a judge met only on Thursdays,
he did not find this position onerous. Finally King Henry VIII forced
him to become a member of the Royal Court. So here we meet one of
the so-called Oxford Reformers. Very funny, isn't it?[1]

---

[1] W. E. Campbell, *op. cit.*, pp. 79-83.

CHAPTER IX

The Grand Tour of Italy

For many years Erasmus yearned to travel in Italy, for that was the home of the wonderful Renaissance! Moreover, in this fascinating land had lived such famous writers as Ovid, Livy, Horace, Cicero, and Sallust. Rome had been for centuries the center of the civilized world. For had not the Gospel of Luke proclaimed that Augustus passed a decree saying that "all the world should be taxed"? Erasmus also had some private matters in mind which made a trip to Italy absolutely necessary. First of all he hoped through the intervention of a powerful friend to obtain a doctorate at the University of Turin. And secondly, he wanted a benefice in England that could not be had for a person like him because of his illegitimate birth. In short, he needed a dispensation from Pope Julius II.

Fortunately for him he was offered a fine position by John Baptist Boerio, the Italian physician of Henry VII, who was anxious to have Erasmus tutor his two sons John and Bernard while they would be traveling in Italy. They had already obtained the services of a tutor named Clifton, and thus Erasmus would be relieved of certain menial tasks. It did not take long to reach Turin, and in this beautiful capital of Savoy the local university would soon be willing to grant Erasmus his highly valued diploma. It was dated September 4, 1506, and indicated that he received the degrees of master and doctor in theology.[1]

His next move was to do some research at the famous University of Bologna, where he spent about one year. He witnessed one day a wonderful spectacle in the form of a huge parade in honor of Pope Julius. But instead of staring at the warlike pontiff with great respect, he reported that he was scandalized by seeing the Vicar of Christ "celebrating bloody triumphs and surveyed the whole thing with a silent groan."[2] Preserved Smith goes on as follows: "His deep hatred and

---

[1] D. Erasmus, *Epistolae Familiares ad Bonifacium Amerbachium* (1779), No. 1.
[2] P. Smith, *op. cit.*, p. 106.

contempt for the man who thus demoralized the Church found expression, a few years later, in a satiric dialogue in which Julius is represented as seeking in vain admission to heaven on the ground that his military exploits had aggrandized the Roman Church." Here Smith is completely mistaken. We have discussed this matter to some extent in our first chapter, and now we must investigate the progress Erasmus made in obtaining further favors from Julius II.

At this point we must listen to the significant remark by Erasmus of his meeting with Cardinal Grimani at the time when this highly influential legate in England enabled Erasmus to win favors from Pope Julius II and the University of Turin. Erasmus said this: "After my first interview with your Eminence, which was also my last, I was prevented from paying you another visit." A strange circumstance had deterred Erasmus from doing what he had intended to do: "I will tell you in plain words and frankly, as becomes a German." He should have said: "As becomes a Dutchman." Then he goes on as follows: "At that time I had quite determined to go to England, to which I was attracted by the sentiment of old acquaintance, by the promises of powerful friends, and by the favor of the most prosperous of kings. I had made this island my adopted country and chosen it for the residence of my old age."[1] Here we might ask Erasmus what made him change his mind.

He remained only for about one year, although much longer than he had done during his first visit in the year 1499. At any rate he was extremely fond of Rome: "I cannot but be touched with a longing for Rome." He was overwhelmed by the favors shown to him by several distinguished cardinals, notably "his Eminence of Nantes, the Cardinal of Bologna, and the Cardinal of St. George; and above all of that most happy colloquy with you." And so he hurried away from Grimani's presence, "and flew rather than travelled to England."

On p. 185 we note that Erasmus had become disappointed with the most recent developments. King Henry VIII had become involved in warfare, and now the great humanist was disturbed. He referred to his earliest patrons: "William, Lord Mountjoy, the earliest patron after Henry of Bergen, bishop of Cambrai." Mountjoy had been, as we saw, a pupil of Erasmus in Paris. Erasmus describes him as follows: "He is a patron of ancient lineage and of incredible goodness to men of letters, but as compared with other barons of this country, is richer in mind than in fortune."

---

[1] *The Epistles of Erasmus*, ed. by Nichols (Russell & Russell, Vol. II), p. 183.

Thanks to Cardinal Grimani and other friends, Erasmus prevailed upon Pope Julius II to absolve him from the guilt of his father in giving him an illegitimate birth. Smith himself admits that Erasmus was getting along very well with "Domenico Grimani, who with 18,000 ducats a year, received the humanist affably."[1] Furthermore, he met Raphael Riario, Cardinal of St. George, "one of the most powerful men at Rome. He also met Cardinal de Medici, later Clement VII." But Smith did not understand the relation between Julius II and Erasmus in the period from 1506 to 1509, when he traveled widely in Italy. However, he did mention the two orations by Erasmus which contradicted each other, one being in favor of a war with Venice and the other one against that policy. "Though the author put more heart into the plea for peace, the other won the day." Erasmus spoke well of his visit to Rome, as Smith showed: "Had I not torn myself from Rome, I could never have resolved to leave. There one enjoys sweet liberty, rich libraries, the charming friendship of writers and scholars, and the sight of antique monuments. I was honored by the society of eminent prelates, so that I cannot conceive of a greater pleasure than to return to the city."[2]

In the year 1937 a certain book appeared in Germany that gave the death-knell to the theory advanced by many eminent European and American scholars, including Preserved Smith, who believed that Erasmus was the author of a notorious dialogue entitled, "Julius Excluded." It was written by Carl Stange and entitled, *Erasmus und Julius II eine Legende* (Berlin: Alfred Töpelmann). The latter explained at great length that Faustus Andrelini, rather than Erasmus, was the author. His strongest point is the fact, as even Roland H. Bainton admitted in his article in the Festschrift honoring Franz Lau (Berlin, 1967),[3] that on the title-page in the original edition the three initials for Andrelini's name are given explicitly: "F[austi] A[ndrelini] F[oroliviensis] Poete Regij libellus de obitu Julij Pontificis Maximi Anno domini M. D. XIII."

The present writer in the introduction to the second edition of his book on young Erasmus has added several other arguments advanced by Stange. In the first place, Huizinga in his famous biography of Erasmus erred in pulling out of its context a statement by Erasmus to the effect that he hated Pope Julius II because Erasmus was opposed to warfare. The Dutch humanist, however, in writing to Anton of Bergen, merely intimated that the war between Venice and Julius II was one instance

[1] P. Smith, *op. cit.*, p. 113.
[2] *Ibidem*, p. 115.
[3] R. H. Bainton, *op. cit.*, pp. 17-25. We shall refer below again to this article by Bainton.

of wars in general, to which nearly all sensible persons were opposed. In certain cases a war for the sake of obtaining liberty was justified, like that fought by Julius II in his efforts to free the rest of Italy from domination by Venice. On May 21, 1515, Erasmus wrote to Pope Leo X that Julius II had been a distinguished pontiff: "Ut maximum declarit Iulium totus paene orbis." Very devastating also is the reference by Stange about the illegitimate birth of Erasmus, who obviously did not want to bring up such a subject in attacking any pope. Every time insinuations were made about his own experience, he cringed with fear and shame.[1] How then could he have been so stupid as to compare his bad luck with that of a pope? Andrelini was exactly the right kind of a person to hint at the desire on the part of Julius II to acquire "gorgeous whores, the most accommodating pimps." While Erasmus was currying favor from Julius II he was not likely to say this about Julius II: "So few come to this place [Rome], when pestilences like this sit at the helm of the Church." Why would a pope reward Erasmus for such ghastly insinuations?[2]

Erasmus learned later on what Luther said about the publication of *Julius Excluded*. Preserved Smith has an amusing tale about this matter. He writes as follows: "Apparently written not long after the death of Julius II (February 21, 1513), it was first published in 1517."[2] However, we have just studied the title-page of the edition issued in 1513. Smith believes that "it was at once attributed to Erasmus, by Scheurl, by Pirckheimer, and by Luther . . . Luther judged it 'so jocund, so learned, and so ingenious – that is, so Erasmian – that it makes the reader laugh at the vices of the Church.'"[3]

Now let us examine the dispensation which Pope Julius II granted to Erasmus on January 4, 1506. The latter's purpose had been to obtain a benefice in England, for which reason he had to have first of all the dispensation just mentioned. It was obviously secured through the efforts of certain English and Italian friends. The kind pope wrote as follows: "Your zeal for religion, honesty of life and character, and other laudable merits, probity, and virtue, for which you have been commended to us by faithful testimony, have induced us to show you special grace and favor." This favor amounted to an absolution from all defects inherent in illegitimacy and the right to hold certain benefices in England. Those

---

[1] A. Hyma, *op. cit.*, 1968 ed., pp. IX-X.
[2] A. Hyma, *op. cit.*, pp. XIII-XIV.
[3] P. Smith, *op. cit.*, pp. 127-128.

who harp upon the hatred which Erasmus felt toward Julius II must have been suffering from a strange hallucination.[1]

It seems also that the recent biographers of Erasmus have not done justice to the labors performed by him in the great port of Venice. The war between Venice and Julius II was of course very disturbing to Erasmus and his friends in England. It seemed to overshadow the tremendous activity on the part of Erasmus in the home of the famous publisher. The capable scholar named William E. Campbell quotes an appropriate statement from the pen of the strange humanist from Holland: "In Italy at present studies are singularly chilled, while wars are warm. Pope Julius fights, conquers, triumphs, and in fact plays the part of Julius to perfection."[2] Campbell also presents useful information about Erasmus' activities in Bologna, where he was so fortunate as to get rid of the incompetent tutor named Clifton. The two pupils were delighted and now, says Campbell, Erasmus "was able to make friends with Paul Bombasio, Professor of Latin and Greek in the University, of whom he speaks as a delightful companion. He also got to know Scipio Fortiguerra, with whom, two years later, he was to spend some very pleasant days in Rome."

Campbell is also correct in telling us that Erasmus' "chief preoccupation throughout the year 1507 was the preparation of the new edition of the *Adagia*." That book of his meant much more to him than the spectacular activities of Pope Julius II. By the year 1507 "he had sufficient Greek to add to the collection both from Greek and Latin, and his commentary, too, was proportionately enlarged, so that finally his collection made a fine folio volume. Its publication in Italy, where it could be properly appreciated, was of high importance, bringing him widespread fame. It became, too, a well of classics, undefiled from which future generations could draw at will. Finally, it brought him the friendship of Aldus Manutius, the founder at Venice in 1494 of the famous Aldine Press. It was fortunate that these two great men should meet; for in addition to an equal taste for the classics, they had also in common a great enthusiasm for the publication of an edition of the New Testament as worthy in scholarship as it was in type."

Campbell also describes for us the meeting between these two giants in the field of world literature. Aldus had languished in prison as the result of the ridiculous war, but finally he was set free, and now he and

---

[1] P. S. Allen, *op. cit.*, Vol. III, p. xxix, ep. 1872.
[2] W. E. Campbell, *op. cit.*, p. 43.

Erasmus became partners in a big enterprise. Aldus had been living with his father-in-law at San Paterniano, near the Rialto Bridge; and "here Erasmus remained for ten months, working at various projects, the most important of all being the second edition of his *Adagia*." In September 1508 the work was finally completed. It was a tribute to the glory of Venice in its dying days as the greatest port in the whole world. Antwerp was now taking its place, as Erasmus well knew. He now hastened to go to Padua (Padova), where he found a most agreeable young man, the illegitimate son of King James IV of Scotland. Although he was now only eighteen years old, he happened to be already the Archbishop of St. Andrews. When further warlike activities threatened to disturb the whole population, the two men went to Siena. But they stopped for a few days in Ferrara, where Erasmus spent a most happy time in the company of Richard Pace, "who was on a diplomatic mission." Moreover, he also had some pleasant talks with Professor Bombasio at Bologna. He spent about two months in Siena, looking after his young pupil. Little did he know then that the latter and his father would be slain four years later in the battle at Flodden Field. He also made a trip to Rome soon after this, but there he did not remain long at this time.

However, his meeting with Cardinal Guiliano Medici, the later Pope Leo X, was naturally of the utmost importance for both men. Campbell reports that Erasmus "was graciously received at his house." At Good Friday, April 6, 1509, the two men from the North were back in Siena. On April 30 they were once more in Rome. Suddenly, however, the archbishop from Scotland was recalled to his native land, and now the whole situation was dramatically changed. Moreover, King Henry VII died on April 22, 1509. After that Lord Mountjoy wrote Erasmus a letter, saying that he must rush back to England, where he would be received with the utmost cordiality. Consequently, he did not remain much longer in Rome than was strictly necessary.

The present writer for many years believed that Erasmus did actually "rush back to England as soon as he received the news of the king's death." He had studied with great respect the excellent biography of Colet by J. H. Lupton. And so in his article on Erasmus and the Oxford Reformers from 1503 to 1519, published in the year 1951 in *Nederlandsch Archief voor Kerkgeschiedenis*, he stated on its first page that Lupton had been correct in giving proper credit to Italy for having made the study of the Greek classics available to the countries North of the Alps. We certainly must not lose sight of the fact that "the universities north of the Alps were, in Colet's time, far behind those in the Peninsula." Lupton indicated that no entire Greek book issued from the Parisian presses till 1507, and none in England till 1543, "while one press in Milan printed a complete Greek book in the year 1476." These figures speak a simple tale. They show where the demand for Greek books resulted in the publication of such books.

F. Seebohm erred grievously in going from one extreme to another. He actually claimed that Colet's lectures on St. Paul were a novelty "in the close of the Middle Ages." He also argued that "the Bible was not free." According to him and his admirer, William E. Campbell, lectures on the Bible were thrown into the background by the much greater relative importance of the lectures on the *Sentences* of Peter Lombard. Christianity was now in its most corrupt form. The Bible had almost ceased to be a record of events, and scholasticism had led men like Erasmus into "a condition of mind in which they practically ignored the Scriptures altogether."[1] But John Colet was different. He boldly began to lecture on parts of the Bible. In this manner he won the respect of Erasmus, who suddenly realized that he had never known what Christianity really was. The present writer on p. 66 of his article in the Dutch magazine just mentioned said this: "For example, the learned W. E. Campbell in his book on Erasmus, Tyndale and More, published in 1949, considers Seebohm a superb guide."[2]

One of the best accounts of the Renaissance in England was written by W. F. Schirmer in his study entitled, *Der englische Frühhumanismus*. He showed that the English humanists formed a small circle, which through their travels in Italy maintained the connection with the source of humanism. Their individual examples were not able to plant in England a real humanistic school. While on the Continent, Wessel Gansfort, Rudolph Agricola, and Alexander Hegius produced a firmly rooted humanism, the English had to wait for another generation. However, the present writer regrets that on p. 67 of his article a serious error appears. There we read that "in the city of Deventer alone some 450 classical works were published before the year 1500." As we have stated above, the total number was nearly 600 and the number of classical books close to 100.

The background of Erasmus in the Netherlands is so little understood that even the great master at Oxford, P. S. Allen, believed, without

---

[1] F. Seebohm, *The Oxford Reformers: Being a History of the Fellowwork of John Colet, Erasmus, and Thomas More* (London, 1867), pp. 1-20.

[2] W. E. Campbell, *op. cit.*, p. 15.

investigating the fact, that the monastery of Steyn near Gouda, where Erasmus was a monk for several years, belonged to the Congregation of Windesheim. Consequently, the Belgian scholar E. de Moreau, S. J. in the fourth volume of his *Histoire de l'Eglise en Belgique* makes the same error. He shows so little interest in the admirable works of Professor J. Lindeboom in Groningen that he calls him Lindemans.[1] That being the case in Great Britain and Belgium, what can we expect from the American scholars? Thus it happened naturally that the present writer himself had Erasmus rushing back to England much too fast.

There was one cardinal in Rome whom Erasmus favored highly. It was Raffaelo Riario, Cardinal of San Giorgio-in-Velabro, a nephew of Pope Julius II, who lived in the sumpuous building known later as the Cancelleria. It was he who asked Erasmus to write two orations about the war between Venice and Pope Julius II, which we have just mentioned above. But those must not be confused with the dialogue entitled, *Julius Excluded*. Erasmus in the spring of 1509 also conferred much with Domenico Grimani, Cardinal of St. Mark, who was then living in the splendid Palazzo di Venezia built by Paul II. When the Cardinal de Medici became pope in the year 1513, he begged Erasmus to return to Rome.[1]

It is obvious that Erasmus in the year 1509 was not hostile to his own friends in Rome, to whom he owed much. He had hoped to accomplish a great deal in Italy, but then his most powerful friends after all were living in England. One important reason for his trip to Italy was to obtain a doctorate at the University of Turin and a dispensation from Pope Julius II. Even when Leo X begged him to return to Rome, he did not have a chance to gain as much advantage in Italy as in England. And the same was true of conditions in his own native land. Lord Mountjoy was still a powerful personage in London, while John Colet and Thomas More also were in a good position to help him obtain all sorts of favors from More's former pupil, now known as King Henry VIII. We have tried in the present chapter to make up for the strange manner in which P. S. Allen slighted the trip to Italy by concluding, as Campbell reported, that "it need not detain us long."[2]

---

[1] E. de Moreau, *op. cit.*, Vol. IV (Brussels, 1949, pp. 149, 283.
[1] W. E. Campbell, *op. cit.*, p. 50.

CHAPTER X

Thomas More and Erasmus

At the end of September 1509 Erasmus left Rome, heading for the Splügen Pass, in order to cross the Alps there on his way to Chur in Switzerland, then Constance and Strasbourg; after which he followed the course of the Rhine to the Low Countries, turning west toward Antwerp. He naturally stopped for a while in Louvain. Preserved Smith wrote as follows: "That Erasmus did not settle in Italy was due to the high hopes of preferment held out to him by English friends on the accession of Henry VIII to the throne on May 22, 1509."[1] This date proves that he was in no rush while in Rome to join his friends in England for the third time. He spent the whole summer somewhere else, meaning in Italy of course.

While he was waiting in the home of Thomas More for his books to arrive, he composed his most famous book, *In Praise of Folly*. He was powerfully affected by Thomas More. This happened during his third visit to England, which lasted for five years (1509-1514). Several distinguished theologians in the United States have reasoned that Erasmus spent all of those five years at Cambridge. For this reason Professor Roland H. Bainton in his biography of Erasmus made the following statement: "Two of the years spent by Erasmus at Cambridge present a riddle. From December 1508 to April 1511 we have not a single letter from his pen."[2]

---

[1] P. Smith, *op. cit.*, p. 116.
[2] R. H. Bainton, *op. cit.*, p. 103. He argues there that Erasmus had to be very cautious in attacking Pope Julius II, "because only popes can grant dispensations from certain canonical regulations and Erasmus stood in need of dispensations." On p. 18 of his article in the Festschrift in honor of Professor Franz Lau (Berlin, 1967), he said: "Sowards suggests very cogently that the reason for the gap is that Erasmus called in and destroyed the letters precisely because they reeked with jibes at Julius which would be quite compromising to one in England after Henry VIII had entered the wat on the side of the pope." Bainton refers here to the article by Sowards (whose initials he wrongly gives as T.K.) in *Studies in the Renaissance*, Vol. IX (1962), pp. 181-196. This is

Now it so happens that one of the most important letters ever composed by Erasmus was dated June 9, 1510. It was written "in the country". An excellent translation was issued by Francis Morgan Nichols in Vol. II of his admirable set of epistles by Erasmus. Here we read this: "Well, the first thing that struck me was your surname of More, which is just as near the name of *Moria* or Folly." Significant is the following remark: "In the next place I surmised, that this playful production of our genius would find special favour with you, disposed as you are to take pleasure in jests of this kind." He was referring to his most famous book, which was written in More's house, namely, *In Praise of Folly*. His letter was intended as the preface to the book in question. The date of this letter has been given variously as June 9, 1508, or 1510, or 1511.[1] Erasmus made fun of many sorts of persons in such a clever manner that most were immensely amused and also determined to correct the numerous abuses in Church and State. We must call attention here to the report by Preserved Smith as published in his fine biography of Erasmus: "During the author's lifetime the *Folly* was printed in nine different cities, and in each of two of them, Venice and Cologne, by three separate publishers. The New Testament was printed by seven publishers in Basel alone." Smith added this comment: "*The Praise of Folly* won an immediate success. Its publication marked the real beginning of that immense international reputation that put its author on a pinacle in the world of letters hardly surpassed or even approached by anyone later save Voltaire."[2]

simply a hallucination on the part of Sowards. He is discussing the contents of letters he had never seen.

[1] Nichols writes as follows on p. 4 of Vol. II: "The above date, Ex *rure Quinto Idus Iunias*, without the year, is found in the first edition, and also in other early editions of the *Moria*, as in those printed by Schürer at Strasburg, in August 1512 . . . The year date, 1508, which is found in later editions, was added afterwards with the usual carelessness . . . That which I have substituted is right, if, as I assume, the Epistle was written as a preface to the *Moria* at the time when the Author was preparing for its first publication by the Press." We gather that Erasmus was living somewhere "in the country," meaning no doubt near London. Nichols argues correctly that it would have made no sense if the author had written a letter to More while he was living in the latter's house. Consequently, he had not yet gone to live in that house, but rather once more in that of Lord Mountjoy at Bedwell, which was indeed "in the country," as we have seen above. During his first trip to England he had first gone to Bedwell, and next to another house at Greenwich, where he had met More. And during the second one he spent several months in that very same house, as we saw. At this point we must not overlook the fact that it was Mountjoy who had induced Erasmus to leave Italy, because he could expect to receive favors from the new king (Henry VIII).

[2] P. Smith, *Erasmus*, p. 125.

We may safely add, however, that Voltaire did not surpass Erasmus. On the contrary, he was vastly overshadowed by Erasmus. The latter was quoted and consulted by the highest potentates in the field of both religion and politics. But on the other hand, he was hated and detested by many kinds of critics. Moreover, his unfair condemnation of scholasticism until nearly the end of his life was not to his credit. What he should have done in 1525 was to return to the Low Countries and make peace with the leading professors in the University of Louvain.

What they had resented most of all was the following passage in *The Praise of Folly*: "St. Peter had the keys of heaven given to him, and that by our Saviour himself, who would never have entrusted him except he had known him capable of their management and custody; and yet it is much to be questioned whether Peter was sensible of the subtlety broached by Scotus, that he may have the key of knowledge effectually, for others who has no knowledge actually in himself. Again, they baptized all nations, and yet never taught what was the formal, material, efficient, and final cause of baptism, and certainly never dreamt of distinguishing between a delible and an indelible character in this sacrament."

"They worshipped in the spirit, following their master's injunction, 'God is a spirit and they who worship must worship in spirit and in truth;' yet it does not appear that it was ever revealed to them how divine adoration should be paid at the same time to our blessed Saviour in heaven and to his picture here below on a wall, drawn with arms extended, two fingers held out, a bald crown, and a circle round his head. . . . St. Paul, who in the judgment of others is no less the chief of the apostles than he was in his own the chief of sinners, who being bred at the feet of Gamaliel, was certainly more eminently a scholar than any of the rest, yet he often exclaims against vain philosophy, warns us from debating about questions and strifes of words, and charges us to avoid profane and vain babblings, and opposition of science, falsely so called. However, our scholastic divines are so modest that if they meet with any passage in St. Paul, or any other penman of Holy Writ, not modeled or critically disposed of as they could wish, they will not roughly condemn it, but bend it rather to a favorable interpretation, out of reverence to antiquity, and to respect to the Holy Scriptures; though indeed it were unreasonable to expect anything of this nature from the apostles, whose lord and master had given them to know the mysteries of God, but not those of philosophy.

"If the same divines meet with anything of like nature unpalatable in

St. Chrysostom, St. Basil, St. Jerome, or others of the Fathers, they will not hesitate to appeal from their authority, and even to resolve that they lay under a mistake. Yet these ancient Fathers were they who confuted both the Jews and the Heathen, though they both obstinately adhered to their respective prejudices; they confuted them, I say, yet rather by their virtuous lives and good works than by words and syllogisms . . . If my judgment be taken, I would advise Christians, in their next expedition to a holy war, instead of those many unsuccessful legions which they have hitherto sent to encounter the Turks and the Saracens, that they would furnish out their clamorous Scotists, their obstinate Occamists, their invincible Albertists, and all their forces of tough, crabbed, and profound disputants."[1]

This is the way Erasmus wrote in the year 1509, under the influence of Thomas More, the author of *Utopia*. In this ideal state described by More, the church pastors were women picked in a public election, the slaves who refused to work were executed, and divorces were freely given to those men and women who could not get along with each other. Moreover, those families who did not have enough children were encouraged to take some from other families, while public restaurants were favored above dining rooms in private homes. In other words, the sanctity of the Christian home was demolished by More and his friends in London. But finally Erasmus got tired of his campaign against the followers of Thomas Aquinas, Duns Scotus, and Albertus Magnus. After the year 1532, as we shall see below, he retreated and returned to the ideals preached in the dormitory attached to the Sorbonne in Paris. Whereas he had ridiculed this dormitory in a colloquy published in the year 1522, he now withdrew his adverse criticism. Unfortunately his critics in Rome and Paris paid no attention to his conversion in the year 1533, and so in the notorious Index of 1559 all of his publications were severely condemned.

In the year 1949 Professor H. V. S. Ogden at the University of Michigan published an edition of *Utopia* in which he stated that the thought of *Utopia* is thoroughly Christian.[2] The fact that all atheists in that strange land were condemned to death by the national government did not disturb that distinguished member of the Department of English. He also believed that those who were ill in Utopia and were forced to be treated in public hospitals were much better off than those who were

---

[1] A. Hyma, *Erasmus and the Humanists*, (New York, 1930), pp. 92-94.
[2] H. V. S. Ogden, *Utopia by Thomas More* (New York: Crofts). See p. viii.

cured in religious institutions. Equally disturbing is the report by Russell Ames in a book entitled, *Citizen Thomas More and His Utopia*. He argues that the kind of Christianity preferred by the Utopians was that of "Colet and Pico and Savonarola and Erasmus."[1] Those scholars who still believe with Preserved Smith that More had in mind a discussion of his own experiences in England should note carefully that the book was written for the most part in the home of Peter Gilles, the town clerk of Antwerp. It was published in what is now Belgium. The second edition appeared in Paris, with an introduction in front addressed to Gilles. Nor did More support orthodox Christianity when he and Erasmus in 1506 published a book in which they supported the views of Lucian, the scoffer. Preserved Smith admits that Lucian "directed his jibes against the man who ascended into heaven." He also says that according to Martin Luther there was a dialogue circulating in Germany entitled, *Lucian on Christ* and ascribed to Erasmus himself.[2]

As for the verdict of Russell Ames, John Colet and Pico della Mirandola seldom agreed with Erasmus in matters of mysticism, while Savonarola was the antithesis of Erasmus in almost every aspect of the orthodox Christian faith and life.[3] It was only after 1532 that Erasmus supported the views entertained by Savonarola and Pico. When in July 1936 the present writer read his paper on Erasmus and the Oxford Reformers in Rotterdam, he was not yet aware of the enormous change in the religious life and thought of Erasmus after 1532. Unfortunately the numerous references made by Erasmus to Christian theology have thus far been neglected by numerous writers. It was not until the year 1966 that a large book was published which devoted adequate space to this important subject: Ernst-Wilhelm Kohls, *Die Theologie des Erasmus* (Basel). Bainton rendered a valuable service to present-day scholarship by calling proper attention to it in his intriguing lecture before the American Council of Learned Societies in January 1967. This august body published the lecture in May 1968 as a separate work which deserved suitable credit.

Unfortunately we cannot attribute to Preserved Smith a similar compliment in analyzing his dicussion of the manner in which Thomas More composed his famous work known as *Utopia*. He argued that the

---

[1] Published by the University of Princeton Press in 1949, See p. 147.
[2] P. Smith, *Erasmus*, p. 194.
[3] A. Hyma, "Erasmus and the Oxford Reformers," in *Bijdragen voor Vaderlandsche Geschiedenis en Oudheidkunde*, Vol. 7 (1936), pp. 141-147.

sources of this amusing treatise "were neither Plato's *Republic* nor the writings of Roman and Christian publicists, but his own experiences as lawyer, judge, and government officer." In other words, Lucian had made a very slight contribution, while even Plato had exerted practically no influence on the composition of *Utopia*.[1] We can show that More's work as an attorney in London did not contribute much to the nature of this mediocre piece of humanistic literature. It should be noted here that around the year 1530 More wished that it would never be translated into English, lest great harm could result for the English people.

---

[1] P. Smith, *op. cit.*, p. 89.

CHAPTER XI

Professor at Cambridge

It had been Erasmus' aim when traveling in Italy to obtain a benefice in England, for which reason he took great pains to please Pope Julius II, whose nephew was favorably impressed with the fine scholarship of the Dutch humanist. During the year 1514 Erasmus wrote a long letter to his superior at the monastery of Steyn near Gouda. But once more he refused, saying that he had been most usefully employed at Cambridge. Astonishing is his report about the great fame he had acquired in England. From the time he spent in the home of Thomas More until the day when he returned to the Continent, he enjoyed immense prestige. Imagine how an American scholar should feel today after having been feted by the Queen of Great Britain, the archbishop of Canterbury, and the top scholars of England! And that is exactly what Erasmus was so considered in the year 1514. Unfortunately this subject has never been treated fully until now.

Let us pause for a few moments and listen to his own testimony: "Wherever I have lived . . . I have been esteemed by the most admired and praised by the most approved. And there is no country, whether Spain, or Italy, or England, or Scotland, which has not invited me to its hospitality . . . In Rome there was not one cardinal who did not treat me as a brother, without my soliciting such distinction . . . And this honor was not rendered to wealth, which I do not possess . . . In England there is not a bishop who is not pleased to receive my greetings The King himself shortly before his father's death, when I was in Italy, wrote me a most loving letter with his own hand . . . The Queen has tried to get me as her teacher; and everybody knows that, if I cared to live at the Court, I might heap up as many benefices as I liked . . . The Archbishop of Canterbury, Primate of all England, a good and learned man, treats me with such kindness as if he were my father or my brother. . . . There are two universities here, at Oxford and Cambridge, both of which seek to have me. For I spent several months teaching Greek and Divinity, but without remuneration, and so I have resolved always to do... In London there is Dr. John Colet, dean of St. Paul's, a man who, uniting the highest learning with admirable piety, exerts a great and general influence. It is well known that he has so much affection for me that there is no one whose society he prefers. I say nothing of a host of other personages, not wishing to annoy you by boasting or loquacity... Lord Mountjoy, a baron of this realm and formerly my pupil, gives me yearly a pension of a hundred crowns."[1]

Now we must not hastily assume that Erasmus spent the whole of the period from 1509 to 1514 in England. Mr. Nichols on p. 10 of his second volume of Erasmus' letters informs us that in April 1511 the latter left London for the Continent. "He was able to take advantage of the society and protection of Lord Mountjoy, who was probably bound for the Castle of Hammes (part of the defences of Calais)." On April 27, 1511, Erasmus wrote a letter in Paris. He stated that Mountjoy did not like the Preface to some of the poems he had recently composed, and so he needed the advice of Ammonio, who afterward helped him obtain a valuable dispensation from Pope Leo X. Nichols informs us that Erasmus on May 19, 1511, had not yet left Paris. Near the end of August 1511 he was invited by the Chancellor of the University of Cambridge to start teaching and lecturing there. We saw above that he "spent several months teaching Greek and Divinity."

In January 1514 he returned to London, as his correspondence shows. He wrote a letter to a person named William Gunnell, saying that he had called "in London on my Maecenates, the Archbishop and Mountjoy." Once more we must emphasize the obvious fact that he did not by any means spend the whole period from 1509 to 1514 at Cambridge, notwithstanding the remarks by Bainton in his latest book devoted to the life of Erasmus. Nevertheless, we shall have to recognize the importance of his teaching there, partly because he had thus far turned down some fine positions, notably at the University of Louvain. It won't surprise us to learn that before long he would be happy to accept a second offer there, which is exactly what happened in the year 1517, as we shall see.

---

[1] A. Hyma, *Erasmus and the Humanists* (New York, 1930), pp. 19-21. This material formed a portion of Erasmus' letter to Servatius at Steyn, explaining the reasons why he refused to return to that monastery. He went so far as to allege that if he went back, he would once more have "to attend drinking parties."

We are very fortunate to have at our disposal a splendid book on Erasmus and Cambridge to which we have referred above. Here we learn that the Dutch humanist finally had settled down to the task of being a university professor. When he started teaching, so says our book, "the amount of new building must have been either exhilirating or annoying, according to taste."[1] The next reference to Erasmus' teaching at Cambridge reads as follows: "To continue with Erasmus' course of study. Every schoolboy should be taught to write original letters in Latin, to turn prose into poetry and poetry into prose, to study the oratory of Cicero and Qunitillian, and to translate Greek into Latin." It is illuminating to note on the next page that "the Cambridge version of *De Ratio Studii* was printed in Paris, in July 1512. At the same time Josse Bade printed a more substantial educational work, running to over 140 pages, *De Duplici Copia Verborum Commentarii Duo*; usually referred to briefly as" "*De Copia*: concerning fullness of expression." An excellent article on this valuable book was published in *Essays on the Northern Renaissance*, issued by Ann Arbor Publishers in the year 1968. Its author was a former student of the present writer who wrote his doctoral dissertation on Erasmus and the Oxford Reformers: Jesse K. Sowards.[2] The latter reported that this treatise soon became "the standard work on rhetorical dilation, adopted by virually every school in England as well as by many continental schools. It went through well over a hundred editions in the sixteenth century alone." And as for the other work, *De Ratione Studii*, the present writer, as mentioned above, published the first two editions side by side in his first article on Erasmus and the Oxford Reformers (1932).

Another educational book by Erasmus while he was teaching at Cambridge was entitled, *De Conscribendis Epistolis*, according to our book on Cambridge. It states that the latter work "dates from Erasmus' Paris days. It was originally written in 1498 for Robert Fisher; Erasmus worked over the manuscript when he came to Cambridge, and gave a copy to Henry Bullock; and in 1521 John Siberch printed the book in Cambridge." Moreover, still another educational work by Erasmus while he was teaching at Cambridge was an edition of moral precepts in couplets dating from the third or fourth century and attributed to Cato. It was published at Louvain in 1514. Finally, Erasmus did a good deal of

[1] D. F. S. Thomson and H. C. Porter, *Erasmus and Cambridge* (University of Toronto Press), p. 27.
[2] J. K. Sowards, "Erasmus and the Apologetic Textbook: A Study of the Duplici Copia Verborum ac Rerum." See p. 93 in particular.

work on William Lily's draft of *Libellus de Constructione Octo Partium Orationis*. It was first printed "with no author named by Richard Pynson in 1513, and to appear in at least two hundred editions throughout Europe before the end of the century."[1]

All of the 64 letters written by and to Erasmus while the latter was living in Cambridge have been published and discussed in the book we have mentioned several times thus far. "First," so report the two editors, "there was his impatient interest in Italian affairs. Erasmus, led on by Lord Mountjoy (among others) had hurried from Italy to London on the accession of Henry VIII; and he was conscious, often with some bitterness, that England was 'this country, which I have chosen in preference to Rome.' By February 1512, after his first Cambridge winter, he was 'tortured' by his longing for Rome, with its 'climate, countryside, libraries, walks, and delightful scholarly conversations.'"[2]

During October and November 1511 his Italian friend Ammonio "sent to Cambridge three quite detailed reports on current Italian events... One key to Erasmus' approach to Italian politics was his hatred of Julius II... Erasmus made fun of him in his second surviving Cambridge letter (to (Ammonio) at the end of August 1511... And so Erasmus disapproved of Julius' attempts to 'liberate Italy from the French, to drive them across the Alps bag and baggage, 'not because I love the French but because I hate war'." That being the case, we must examine the degree of hatred which Erasmus is supposed to have cherished for Julius II, according to several authors we have mentioned thus far. First of all we note this revealing remark about Cambridge: "There is absolutely no reason to congratulate me on account of my Cambridge retreat." That we can readily understand. Now there is absolutely nothing on Pope Julius II. The latter's name and activities are not mentioned at all, for it was the French who had sought to occupy Italy, and the pope naturally felt it his duty to defend his own people against foreign invaders. Here then we find one more of the numerous allegations concerning Pope Julius II by persons who have been drawing far more upon their own imaginations than upon historical facts.

It is also illuminating to observe that Ammonio stayed for a while with Thomas More and his first wife in London. The latter died in the summer of 1511. By the end of October More had married again, and now Ammonio remained in this home until October. Evidently, accord-

---

[1] Thomson and Porter, *op. cit.*, pp. 59-61.
[2] *Ibidem*, p. 66.

ing to our book on Cambridge, he soon left, for "the new Mrs. More, Dame Alice Middleton," did not like him. As for Erasmus, we are informed that "some time in July Fisher persuaded Erasmus to accept a position at Cambridge as lecturer in Greek." The Dutch humanist had had two elegant offers before, one from Oxford in 1499 and the other from Louvain in 1502, both of which he had declined. But now he was happy to accept the position, largely because he did not feel at ease in continually accepting hospitality from his English friends.[1]

On or about August 18, 1511, Erasmus left London for Cambridge. As soon as he arrived he engaged the services of a physician. "Fortunately there was a Dutch physician in town, Dr. Bout, whose patent medicines seem to have given him some reputation as an alchemist." Our books tells us that Erasmus had asked Pope Julius II to free him from the stain of his illegitimate birth. First of all he asked in particular for permission to change his clothes: "either to use the habit of my order or to refrain from using it, at my discretion, provided only that I dress lik a cleric." And so "Julius, in a letter, gave him 'a full pardon' for 'any faults I had previously committed in this respect.'" Consequently, "in Italy he wore the costume of a secular priest. When he returned to England in the summer of 1509 he decided (so he said) to wear again the modified Augustinian habit. Julius' dispensation probably applied only to Italy." However, he "packed away his Augustinian garments in a trunk and dressed as an ordinary priest. He was so dressed throughout his Cambridge stay." We also learn that "when he was given the living of Aldington in March 1512, worth about L40 a year, he immediately resigned it for a pension therefrom." But this statement is false, for he kept this benefice for three months, as we shall see below.

And as for the so-called hatred Erasmus felt for Julius II, it must be noted here that "during Nobember 1511, less than three months after Erasmus went to Cambridge, Henry VIII allied himself with the Pope." In the alliance was also King Ferdinand of Aragon, the father-in-law of Henry VIII.[2] And since the latter was a patron of Erasmus, we are getting very concerned about the opinions expressed to the effect that Erasmus must have hated Julius II very much indeed! This is particularly true of the two British scholars who wrote their book on Erasmus at Cambridge.

As for Erasmus' pay at Cambridge, we know that he received less than the total of his own expenses, which amounted to about 100

---

[1] Thomson and Porter, *op. cit.*, pp. 101-102.
[2] Thomson and Porter, *op. cit.*, p. 67.

English pounds a year. He held two lectureships in Greek language and literature. He often complained about those people on the campus "who haven't a rag to their backs." But Ammonio told him correctly that he was rather lucky, because of his powerful patrons. His local colleagues received only about ten pounds a year plus board and room. He "got almost nothing from his students." He also received money from Colet and Fisher, and at the end of 1513 Bishop Ruthall of Durham gave him about fifty shillings. "I am," wrote Erasmus in November 1511, "so far as *promises* are concerned – unmistakably wealthy; apart from which I live in stark hunger." As for his work on the campus, he wrote Colet on September 13, 1511, that he had to battle on Colet's behalf against the Thomists and Scotists.[1] At the end of September or the beginning of October he took a short trip to London in order to talk with his devoted friend Josse Bade, or Badius, a Netherlander who had published in Paris his edition of Valla's notes on the New Testament, his Latin translations from Euripides (1506), and the Erasmus-More translations from Lucian (1506). He stayed in More's house in Bucklersbury, where Ammonio also had a room. He made some useful references to his own teaching in a letter dated October 16, 1511, and addressed to Ammonio: "Up to this moment I have been lecturing on Chrysoloras' Grammar, but the audience is small; perhaps more people will attend when I start Theodore's Grammar. Perhaps also I will undertake lecturing in theology, for that is under discussion at present." Very interesting also is the letter from Ammonio, dated October 27, 1511. He makes an important reference to Julius II: "Pope Julius has gone to the shrine of the Mother of God at Loretto for his health."[1]

Very important is the letter from Erasmus addressed to Ammonio on November 26, 1511. First we note his remark about the visit which Julius II made to the shrine we have just mentioned: "What is this you tell me? *The* Pope gone to Loretto? *What piety!*" Next follows a significant remark about the war which many scholars have used to show that Erasmus hated Julius II: "As to the war that has been set afoot, I am afraid now at last the Greek proverb the *singed moth's doom* may come to pass. For if anything happens to the Roman Church, then who, I ask you, could more properly be blamed for it than the all-too-mighty *Julius*? But pray suppose the French have been driven out of Italy and then reflect, please, whether you prefer to have Spaniards as your masters – or the Venetians, whose rule is intolerable even to their own

---

[1] Thomson and Porter, *op. cit.*, pp. 70-74, 109, 115, 118.

countrymen. Priests are something princes will never put up with; and yet they won't ever be able to agree among themselves because of their worse-than-mortal faction-feuds. I fear Italy is to have a change of masters, and, because she can't endure the French, may have to endure French rule multiplied by two ... I am most delighted that you are Lucianizing, and when you get back to London, that is, before December 13 if heaven so wills, we'll pursue Greek studies together." On November 27, 1511, Erasmus told Ammonio something about the local university that was far from flattering: "And here in Cambridge – what a University! No one can be found who will write even moderately well at any price."[1]

Our book on Cambridge informs us that Erasmus "was in London by the middle of February 1514. He stayed there until the first week in July, which was about five months. At the end of the first week in July 1514 he crossed the Channel to Calais. On July 8 he wrote a letter to the prior at Steyn in which he replied to questions about his recent activities, and discussed his serious illnesses and his refusal to return to Steyn. The present writer in the year 1930 published this letter in his source book on Erasmus entitled, *Erasmus and the Humanists*. A few extracts have been quoted above. From the castle at Hamme he traveled to Saint Omer, Ghent, Antwerp, Louvain, Liège, Strasbourg, Schlettstadt, and then finally to Basel, which he reached at the end of August. Now followed a period of great enjoyment as he prepared his most valuable work, the edition of the New Testament in its original Greek. Modern Christianity is in vast debt to him for this labor.

We have stated above that Erasmus did not immediately give up his benefice. On p. 145 of our book on Cambridge we read that "so Erasmus was in Cambridge for the second half of February 1512. His next letter from the university was nine weeks after Letter 24; for some of that time he was again in London, for at last, after six years of waiting, he had been given an English living: Aldington. The rectory of Aldington, Kent, was in the deanery of Lympne and the diocese of Canterbury, and was in Warham's gift. It was one of the richest livings in the diocese, and the second wealthiest in the deanery ... Erasmus was formally presented to Aldington on March 22, 1512. Within three months, however, he resigned as rector, and the living was taken over by John Thornton, suffragan bishop to Warham." The rector was ordered to pay Erasmus for life an annual pension, amounting to L 15 1 s. 2d.

---

[1] Thomson and Porter, *op. cit.*, pp. 135-136.

Beatus Rhenanus reported that "Erasmus had some scruples at first in accepting, considering that the entire emoluments rather belonged to the pastor, whose business it undeniably was to be present day and night to instruct the people placed under his charge, but the Archbishop met his hesitation with the following question: 'Who, said he, has a fairer claim to live out of a church income than yourself, the one person who by your valuable writings instructs and educates the pastors themselves, and not them alone but all the churches of the world?'"

Our book then goes on as follows: "The official reason for Erasmus' resignation was his ignorance of English. But perhaps a more pressing consideration was his doubt, in view of his illegitimate birth, about his priestly orders. Or did he develop scruples, spurred by Colet's words in the February Convocation Sermon about 'personal residence of curates in their cures?' (But Colet had already attacked pensions.) The pension, at any rate, was his. But how much of it attracted tax?"[1] Further discussion of the details involved follows in our book, which is of little value to us now. So we have learned that Archbishop Warham in England assisted Pope Julius II in helping poor Erasmus to the best of their abilities. It does not seem likely, therefore, that Erasmus one year later composed the notorious dialogue against his own friend in Rome. Moreover, since the original edition issued in 1513 stated that Faustus Andrelini was the author, we might as well "let sleeping dogs alone."

On p. 17 of the source book published by the present writer we observe another confession by Erasmus: "I was never a slave to pleasures, though formerly I was inclined to them." And as for monasticism in general, he wrote as follows: "There are colleges in which there is so much religion and such well-regulated mode of living that, if you saw it, you would think less of any monastic rule." He finally came to the conclusion that the human organs of reproduction must be used only for the process of reproduction, and not for the derivation of physical pleasure. In his *Catechism*, composed after 1531, he wrote: "The chaste married life is some thing dignified, but far more dignified is continuous chastity, if spontaneous and freely undertaken." On several occasions he had expressed the following opinion: "Marriage is a refuge for the weak."

---

[1] Thomson and Porter, *op. cit.*, pp. 146-147.

CHAPTER XII

The Greek New Testament

In London Erasmus started his important work on the Greek New Testament. Professor Preserved Smith at Cornell University devoted a valuable chapter to this fabulous work. He says on p. 161 of his brilliant biography of Erasmus: "He did it under the diverse influences of Colet and Valla, the one aglow with piety, the other as cold as a rationalist ever born." John Colet had been the Dean of St. Paul's Cathedral, as we saw, besides the founder of his school attached to that cathedral. He was for many years a very close friend and admirer of Erasmus. Since the New Testament is by far the most important piece of literature the human race has ever known, we are naturally prone to note what the great humanist from Rotterdam did with it. Preserved Smith has this comment: "There was no standard edition of it, manuscripts and printed books differing from each other." Erasmus was well aware of this, and he took upon himself the task of establishing the first authentic text.

Although John Colet was not able to perform the task himself, he delivered some learned lectures on the Apostle Paul at his school and church. He kept on urging Erasmus to perform a task that really was beyond Colet's capacity. Thus inspired by the English dean Erasmus searched for the best copies in the Greek language. In the Premonstratensian Abbey of Park near Louvain he found Valla's *Notes on the New Testament*, which had not yet been printed. This happened in the year 1504, and during the month of December in that year he published this daring attack upon the old and highly respected text of the Bible known as the Vulgate. Preserved Smith grows very eloquent as the proceeds thus on p. 161: "The work was more important than is generally realized . . . It was the skeptic Valla that first disclosed the true, sound method of exegesis, and thus uncovered the long-hidden meaning. The cock had found the pearl; the careless wayfarer had chanced upon the nugget of gold; the scoffer who sought to shame truth by unveiling her had made her more beautiful." The writer has shown in his book published in 1968 that Erasmus in composing the *Book Against the Barbarians* had expressed his profound admiration for Valla. Now, in December 1504 he continued to depend on Valla for further disputes with the highest authorities in the Roman Catholic Church, especially those in Paris.

Preserved Smith informs us that "it was probably at the instigation of Colet that Erasmus began an original Latin version of the New Testament." This task was completed by October 1506. We now know that "the hope of a benefice drew Erasmus to England for the second time in the summer or autumn of 1505." King Henry VII promised him a benefice in a letter addressed to him by himself. It was dated April 1506, and we can give as a reference the publications by both Nichols and Allen. Erasmus came to England early in the spring of 1505. Smith said that "so vivid was Erasmus's expectation of the benefice that he took the trouble to get a dispensation from Pope Julius II to meet any difficulties that might arise from his illegitimacy." The date of this dispensation was January 4, 1506. We might once more indicate that those historians who have been harping on the hatred which Erasmus felt for Julius II were very poorly informed.

In March 1516 Erasmus finally published his world-famous Greek version of the New Testament. It was entitled, *Novum Instrumentum omne, diligenter ab Erasmo Rot. Recognitum et Emendatum*. The publisher was his intimate friend, John Froben, with whom he lodged in the city of Basel for ten months after November 15, 1521. Preserved Smith tells us on p. 181 that the work exerted its greatest influence in Germany soon after it appeared in print: "On the men later to be Reformers the influence of the work was incalculable." Melanchthon "praised it as divinely guided." Moreover, "Ulrich Zwingli bought, transcribed, and annotated a copy with his own hands." And as for Luther, we note that "he apparently secured the new edition at the earliest possible moment, and from that time forth, beginning, namely, with the ninth chapter of the epistle [to the Romans], he took Erasmus as his chief authority in exegesis." Even more important was the influence exerted upon those who translated the new Testament into the vernacular languages. And so Preserved Smith drew this significant conclusion on p. 183: "But the most important service of the Greek New Testament has yet to be mentioned. It was the fountain and source from which flowed the new translations into the vernaculars which like rivers irrigated the dry lands of the mediaeval Church and made them blossom into a more enlightened and lovely form of religion." It is also worth mentioning that John Colet urged Erasmus to "follow up his editorial work with an extended commentary." Consequently, he produced "a number of *Paraphrases* of the books of the New Testament." The first was dedicated to Cardinal Domenico Grimani, who, as we saw, enabled Erasmus to "win favors from Pope Julius II and the University of Turin."

Now we shall depict the background of the Greek New Testament as finally issued by Erasmus in the year 1515. First of all we must follow the activities of the Dutch humanist which led up to the definitive text of his Greek New Testament. The famous Council of Trent (1545-1563) declared officially that the Greek New Testament was simply the Greek translation of the final Latin version in the latter section of the Vulgate. The latter had been put together by Jerome, the capable Church Father who spent much time in Bethlehem. However, his Eminence Johannes Cardinal de Jong stated in the first volume of his admirable work entitled, *Handboek der Kerkgeschiedenis* (Utrecht, Nijmegen, Antwerp, Brussels, and Louvain, 1945), that the translation was not perfect and that St. Augustine regarded it "with suspicion."[1]

Erasmus was well aware of these facts, and so he labored hard in using the notes on the New Testament by Lorenzo Valla, as we noted above. After his third trip to England he was once more active in the Low Countries. But his residence in that area was short. He hastened to Basel in order to supervise the new edition of the *Adages* made by Johann Froben. He was there in August 1514, but the new edition did not appear until the middle of March 1515. Next he returned to England, and so in May we find him working there since the 7th day on his book entitled, *The Christian Prince*, or *The Education of a Christian Prince*. An excellent edition of this brilliant work was published by L. K. Born in 1936 (New York imprint). Thomas More was then on a mission to Flanders. Erasmus wrote that "the two most learned men of all England are now at Bruges."[2] In January 1516 he was appointed Councillor to King Charles of Spain, and it was to him that this fabulous book was dedicated. In March he was back in Basel. We are very fortunate to have now at our disposal a wonderful chapter on this work in the book by Robert P. Adams, whom we have mentioned several times above. It is properly entitled, "The Genius of the Island – Erasmus' Christian Prince (1516)." Adams complains correctly that this book has been shamefully neglected

---

[1] J. de Jong, *op. cit.*, p. 298.
[2] R. P. Adams, *op. cit.*, p. 109.

by various European authors, especially in England. Erasmus emphasized the need of Christian principles in promoting the cause of peace. He bitterly complained about the corrupt policy of Pope Julius II. Since the latter was now dead, the writer could freely express his contempt of warlike activities on the part of this pope. But this does not alter the previous policy pursued by Erasmus around the year 1506, when he badly needed favors, which he received gratefully.[1]

Once more we shall present a useful quotation from the book by R. P. Adams: "As the slow English spring came on in 1517, Archbishop Warham, a power for peace and always Erasmus' best patron in England, longed for Erasmus' conversation to make his retirement more pleasant. Leaving no work for peace undone, before leaving Brussels in April Erasmus hastily wrote to Pope Leo X to congratulate him upon his effective work for peace ... Then he came over to England, for what we now know (although he certainly did not) was to be his last visit."[2] In July he was in Louvain, where he completed a wonderful work entitled, *Complaint of Peace*. He was now starting his career of professor in the local university, and he naturally returned to the field of the Christian religion. In March 1516 he issued his first edition of the Greek New Testament, which naturally appeared in print at Basel, where Johann Froben was still printing several books by Erasmus, especially the *Praise of Folly*. The second edition was published in 1519. He had used ten manuscripts, of which he found four in England and five at Basel. The tenth he got from his valiant friend, John Reuchlin. For the important second edition he employed several more original sources, among which were two from the Augustinian priory near Turnhout, and two from the Monastery of Mount St. Agnes near Zwolle (where Thomas à Kempis had worked on his version of the *Imitation*). In 1520 and 1521 he also used two others in Brussels, besides one in Liège, thus indicating his dependence upon the source materials in the Low Countries. He lived in Louvain most of the time from 1517 to 1521. For the second edition he introduced about 400 alterations. And obviously the manuscripts used in 1520 and 1521 were intended for the third edition.

We observe that for the Apocalypse he employed good sources, but one of his assistants copied the best one so carelessly that" many gross errors" were made, "some of which have been perpetuated for centuries." For example, Chapter XVII, 8 contained a serious error

---

[1] *Ibidem*, pp. 112-115.
[2] R. P. Adams, *op. cit.*, p. 161.

which "crept into Luther's German, where it was first corrected in 1892; and into the Authorized English Bible, which reads, 'is not and yet is.'" And so in the Revised Version we have this: "is not and shall come." Smith also reports that, since the last six verses were lacking altogether in his mss., "Erasmus supplied them by translating the Vulgate into very lame Greek." Smith scornfully states that many recent critics made Erasmus "the butt of endless sarcasm by modern scholars." He was "able, here and there, by means of grammatical and historical knowledge superior to that of his contemporaries, to improve the text by conjectural emendation. His wide reading in the early fathers stood him in good stead not only in elucidating, but in restoring the text."[1]

Very interesting is the comment by Smith about the verse I John v, 7. Here we read this in the Authorized (King James) Version: "For there are three that bear record in heaven, the Father, the Word, and the Holy Ghost: and these three are one." Says Smith: "The verse is an interpolation, first quoted and perhaps introduced by Priscilian (A.D. 380) as a pious fraud to convince doubters of the doctrine of the Trinity. Not finding it in any Greek manuscript, Erasmus properly omitted it; for this honest, practically unavoidable conduct, he was ferociously attacked." Then his enemies forced him to put it back into the version he had made before. And thus, says Smith, "the forged verse was put back into the Greek to be kept there until the nineteenth century."[2]

Another important report by Smith also requires mention here. Erasmus discovered two more interpolations. The first one was by no means a slight affair, for it constituted the last twelve versus of Mark's Gospel. Though he retained them in his text, "he honestly noted that they were doubtful." Equally important were the verses in John VII, 53 to VIII, 11. So Smith continues as follows: "The form in which he left the text was little improved by the labors of Beza and Estienne in the sixteenth century. The edition of 1633, differing little from his, became known as the 'textus receptus,' and was not substantially castigated until the labors of Tischendorf, and of Hort, in the nineteenth century, restored the original on really scientific principles."[3]

---

[1] P. Smith, *op. cit.*, p. 164.
[2] P. Smith, *op. cit.*, pp. 165-166.
[3] P. Smith, *op. cit.*, pp. 166-167.

CHAPTER XIII

Louvain Versus Wittenberg

Erasmus left England for the last time in April 1517, at the end of his fifth trip, expecting to return soon. But during the next four years he chose to remain nearly all the time in the Netherlands, and there chiefly at Louvain, where in the year 1517 he became a professor in the local university. On August 30, 1517, he matriculated as *Magister Erasmus de Roterodamis sacrae theologiae professor*.[1] He enabled some of his friends there to found the celebrated College of the Three Languages, meaning Latin, Greek, and Hebrew. The first financial bequest came from Jerome Busleiden, who had been mentioned, as we saw, in the book published by Erasmus and Thomas More in 1506, containing translations of 32 treatises by Lucian. Professor Henry de Vocht in the year 1954 published the third of four learned volumes in his history of this college under the title of *History of the Foundation and the Rise of the Collegium Trilingue Lovaniense 1517-1550*. There he wrote as follows: "That room, which, in 1520, was constructed to contain three hundred hearers, had become too small within a few years, so that John Stercke had bought on January 28, 1524, part of the premises of a neighbour, ... at any rate, Erasmus could refer, already on April 8, 1525, to the six hundred hearers who regularly gathered in the magnificently constructed room. Three years later, the auditory had become too small again, for Glocenius was obliged to double his lessons, as he announced to Erasmus on May 10, 1528."[2] Surely, audiences of over 1,200 were an eloquent testimony to the success of this humanistic institution!

Charles Béné in his doctoral dissertation presented to the Faculty of Letters and Human Sciences at the University of Paris in the year 1969 included a chapter on the study of the three languages. It is based upon several other chapters which precede it. There we note valuable dis-

[1] P. Smith, *op. cit.*, p. 154.
[2] Henry de Vocht, *op. cit.*, p. 13 of Vol. III.

cussions by the learned writer about the "first defense of the new exegesis: Erasmus and Martin Dorp," which happens to be the title of Chapter V in the section dealing with the Greek Testament produced by Erasmus. It starts as follows: "Erasmus, having left England in July 1514, undoubtedly went to Basel by way of Brabant, where he spent several weeks. There he met once more an old friend, Martin Bartholomew van Dorp, who was 15 years younger than Erasmus." He had probably become well acquainted with Dorp when the latter was studying at the College of the Lily (Lys) in Louvain, between 1502 and 1504. There Dorp became a professor in 1504. Four years later he organized the presentation of two works by Plautus entitled, *Aulularia* and *Miles Gloriosus*. After that he studied theology, and in 1510 he became a member of the University Council. Soon after that he obtained a doctorate in theology, next he became a professor of theology (1515), while in the year 1523 he was promoted to the office of rector.[1]

In September 1514 Dorp wrote Erasmus an important letter in which he discussed several grand projects planned and executed by Erasmus: the *Praise of Folly*, the edition of Jerome's Letters, and the edition of the Greek New Testament. Erasmus responded by defending these three works of his. Next came a letter by Dorp in which he disapproved of the manner in which Erasmus had organized this edition. Strange though it may seem, says Béné, both scholars quoted from St. Augustine in defending their respective positions. Dorp did not mind the edition of Jerome's letters, but he disapproved of *The Praise of Folly* and advised his stubborn friend not to issue a new edition of this scurrilous work. He also was strongly opposed to the idea of getting out another edition of the Greek New Testament. He argued that the Greek version called the Septuagint had been corrupted by heretics. He thus sincerely disagreed with St. Augustine.[2]

Erasmus replied by arguing that the knowledge of the three ancient languages was necessary in determining just what the correct text of the New Testament was. Béné now takes up the positions adopted by A. Renaudet, F. Seebohm, Margaret Mann Phillips, and the present writer.[3] He notes that the famous Lucien Febvre supports M. M. Phillips and A. Hyma.[4] These writers not only found the influence of Colet to

---

[1] Charles Béné, *op. cit.*, p. 207.
[2] Ch. Béné, *op cit*, p 208: "Mais, à propos des sources greques, Dorp n'hésite pas à s'opposer à l'opinion d'Augustin."
[3] Ch. Béné, *op. cit.*, p. 219.
[4] Ch. Béné, *op. cit.*, p. 219, note 25.

have been considerable but gave more credit to the work done by Lorenzo Valla, as far as the edition of the Greek New Testament by Erasmus was concerned. Moreover, Erasmus showed immense respect for Jerome, whose works he issued in the year 1516.[1] We have observed above that the Brethren of the Common Life had made Jerome their patron saint and that their famous school in Liège was called the College of Jerome. They were often called Jeromites. In their house at Gouda the Jerome edition of 1516 was preserved, and so the present writer found a copy in the City Library, with the *Book Against the Barbarians* written on some extra sheets of paper, with the date of 1519 at the bottom. Here is the only copy of the original version of this highly influential book by Erasmus. It is a shame that the Dutch scholars before 1930 ignored this particular version.

Béné tells us correctly that "there is one point on which the critics have agreed just about unanimously, namely, by neglecting or rejecting the influence of St. Augustine."[2] That statement is unfortunately true. He is referring to the influence exerted upon the exegesis of Erasmus. Not only in the preparation of the Greek New Testament but also in shaping several other publications, the Dutch humanist was naturally affected by St. Augustine. Béné repeatedly refers to the edition of the *Methodus* by Hajo Holborn, where St. Augustine is quoted ten times out of a total of fifteen times. Even more remarkable is the situation in the *Ratio Verae Theologicae*, in which St. Augustine is mentioned 48 times and all the other Church Fathers together only 41 times!

As soon as Erasmus was installed as professor in the College of the Lys in the University of Louvain, he suddenly was attacked from many directions. He remained there for three years (1518-1521), and at the very beginning, in the Preface of 1518 in the Greek New Testament, he defended himself against his opponents. Among the latter were Lefèvre, Edward Lee, Pierre Couturier, Noel Beda, and James Zuniga. But especially important was his Apology directed against a scholar named Jacques Masson, or Latomus. The latter was a pupil of John Standonck when he was living in the College of Montaigu at the University of Paris. During the year 1500 his residence was the Home of the Poor in Louvain, and there he remained for nine years. After that he took up the study of theology, attacking Erasmus in his *Dialogue*. He strongly disapproved of the new work by Erasmus, the *Ratio Verae*

---

[1] Ch. Béné, *op. cit.*, p. 219: "Le vrai maître d'Erasme, pour Renaudet, c'est Jérôme."
[2] Ch. Béné, *op. cit.*, p. 220.

Theologiae. But soon a prominent scholar called Peter Schade, and also Peter Mosellanus (named after the river Moselle) came along to defend Erasmus. He was the rector at the University of Leipzig in 1520 and 1523. The *Discourse* by Latomus was widely discussed at the University of Louvain. He and Erasmus urged all scholars to study with great care the three ancient languages. Not only the theologians but also the professors in the faculties of law, medicine, and the liberal arts badly needed the knowledge of those languages, so he reasoned.

Moreover, there appeared upon the scene a notable scholar named Alard of Amsterdam, who on March 6, 1519, tried in vain to give a lecture on the work of Erasmus and the famous Dutch humanist named Rudolph Agricola. It was indicated by the authorities on the campus that he was not a member of the university. But the Vice-Chancellor, John Briart of Ath, supported Jacques Latomus, or Masson, who now came up with a second work called *Dialogue*. The latter acquired much local fame with his *Dialogus de Trium Linguarum et Studii Theologici*, in which he attacked both Erasmus and Mosellanus. He was particularly severe in condemning the publication by Erasmus and More of 32 dialogues of Lucian in 1506, which book we have discussed above. In short, he defended scholastic theology over against that by Erasmus and More. However, he was answered directly by Professor Matthew Adrianus, who taught Hebrew on the local campus and naturally did not relish the attacks by Latomus on the idea of reviving the study of the three ancient languages, notably Hebrew. He warmly supported the fine work done by Pope Leo X, Cisneros, and Busleiden. The next defender was Erasmus, who on March 28, 1519, published a letter in Antwerp without a date on it and in May 1519 at Basel, issued by Froben. There he made it clear that attacks on his method should not be confounded with those on Luther. He emphasized in particular the barbarous style of the leading theologians.[1]

Many scholars have wondered why Erasmus in his biography of John Colet said that the latter was more unfavorable to St. Augustine than to any other ancient writer. The present writer used to think that he committed an error or else deliberately told a lie about his friend. In his lecture delivered in July 1936 at the Erasmus Symposium he made the following statement: "The original version puzzled Lupton greatly, but he could find no other meaning. The statement is indeed a bad puzzle until one observes that in 1521 Erasmus was becoming more and

---

[1] Ch. Béné, *op. cit.*, pp. 281-417.

more hostile to Augustine as Luther grew more respectful toward him." And in the footnote to this presentation as published in the second edition of his book on young Erasmus was added this: "We know that it has become customary to accept almost everything that Erasmus said as the gospel truth ... When he deliberately tells a lie, he knows why he is doing it. In 1521 he had at last come to an open break with Luther, the admirer of Augustine."[1] However, Béné has analyzed a long letter addressed by Erasmus to John Eck in 1518. There he already explains at great length why he greatly prefers Jerome above Augustine. To the latter, so he argued, ancient Hebrew and Greek literature was a closed field of knowledge. "When I was young, I shared your opinion, but I now believe that I have with increasing old age acquired more proper judgment. I admire Jerome much more now." That letter, so concludes Béné, explains his attitude toward Augustine, with his ignorance of the ancient languages, which closed to him Greek and Hebrew literature. Moreover, he was also obviously ignorant in the field of Greek philosophy."[2] Augustine had become the champion of the scholastic philosophers. "Already in his correspondence with Dorp he had stated that Augustine was not the true defender of the ancient literatures and science."

Erasmus' hostility to monasticism appears in the following statement written on April 5, 1518, and addressed to Marcus Laurinius: "But look now, how Christian this proceeding is, how worthy of their profession as Monks, – to tear in tatters before an unlearned audience the reputation of another (which they cannot repair if they wished to do so), when all the while they know nothing at all about the matter with which they find fault."[3] His opposition to wars in general should be carefully studied by those who still imagine that he hated Julius II in particular: "At every Prince's Court masked Theologians are dominant. The Roman Curia is incapable of a blush, for what can be more shameful than this constant supply of Pardons? The pretext is now put forward of a war against the Turks."[4] As for his work on the local campus, we have this statement written on October 31, 1517: "We are now living in the Lilian College with the kindest of hosts, Naef of Hontescote; and I have now become quite *Magister noster*, taking a frequent part in

---

[1] A. Hyma, *The Youth of Erasmus*, 1968 ed., p. 352.
[2] Ch. Béné, *op. cit.*, pp. 338-339.
[3] Erasmus, *Letters*, ed. by F. M. Nichols, Vol. III (New York reprint, Russell & Russell, 1962), p. 323.
[4] Erasmus, *Letters*, III, p. 298.

all the University Acts."¹ In September 1517 he wrote this about his university: "I find the divines of Louvain candid and courteous, especially Atensis, the Chancellor of the University, a man of incomparable learning and singular kindness. There is no less theological erudition here than in Paris, but there is less sophistry and conceit."²

We must be careful not to assume that Erasmus from July 1517 to the first half of July 1521 was living all the time in Louvain. For example, one letter was written at Antwerp on May 18, 1517; and Mr. F. M. Nichols, the editor, published near the end of it the following report on p. 412 of Vol. III: "Basel, 31 May, 1518." On p. 428 we have this: "Basel, 23 August, 1518." On top of p. 377 we read: "Four Epistles written at Antwerp in the year 1517, and not included in previous chapters." And in the chronological register in front of Vol. III Nichols has this note on Basel for eight letters composed there by Erasmus with these dates on them: 31 May, 1518 (twice); August 1518; 26 July, 1518; 23 August, 1518; 26 August, 1518; 31 August, 1518.

During the year 1521 Erasmus gradually became hostile to his colleagues in the University of Louvain, for which reason in part he moved to Basel, where Johann Froben was publishing several books of his. In Louvain, on the other hand, the local printing business was relatively poor and small. Consequently, he lived in Froben's home for ten months, starting with November 15, 1521. At the same time he also turned against Luther. On May 10, 1521, he wrote a long letter to Justus Jonas, a close friend and supporter of Luther. He said that Luther had "gradually alienated good men by his passion, by his railing against the pope, against the friars, against the universities, and against Aristotle's philosophy."³ Luther, so he argued, would have done better to have thrown himself on the mercy of pope and emperor. In another letter addressed to Duke George of Saxony, dated September 3, 1523, he referred to the attack by King Henry VIII of England on Luther: "I have never doubted that the book of the Serene King of England, which you praise with good reason, was the work of him whose name it bears... When he was a boy he carefully studied my writings, at the suggestion of William Mountjoy, a former pupil of mine, whom he made his intimate friend."⁴

Erasmus for eighteen months had carried on a lively correspondence,

---

1 *Ibidem*, p. 118.
2 *Ibidem*, p. 79.
3 P. Smith, *op. cit.*, p. 247.
4 A. Hyma, *New Light on Martin Luther* (Ann Arbor, Mich., 1958), p. 153.

trying to heal the breach between Luther and his opponents. He took great pains from 1517 to 1524 to defend Luther on many occasions. It seems rather surprising to study some of his letters during that period, and the present writer in some of his publications has quoted large excerpts from them. Erasmus reasoned as follows: "Only two universities had condemned Luther, and in many others he had received powerful support. The persecution suffered by him was caused chiefly by a hatred of learning and a love of tyranny. In a series of propositions called *Axioms* he set forth his own position. This annoyed many of his former friends in Louvain, for which reason he left the Netherlands."

His final breach with Luther came in 1525, when Luther wrote a savage attack on Erasmus for having expressed certain strong opinions in his work entitled, *On the Free Will*. It was published shortly before September 6, 1524, when Erasmus wrote two letters about it to Melanchthon and Duke George of Saxony. On May 21, 1524, the latter had written Erasmus as follows: "I wish that God had put it into your mind three years ago to separate yourself from the Lutheran faction." He blamed the famous scholar for having waited too long, for "it would have been much easier to quench a spark than to put it out now." So in September he finally explained his course of action: "I had a triple array of enemies. The theologians and haters of letters were leaving no stone unturned to destroy Erasmus, not only because they had been attacked in my books, but because I had entered their flourishing University of Louvain and infected the whole region." The present writer has devoted a long chapter to this controversy in his book published by Eerdmans (Grand Rapids, Mich.) in 1958 and entitled, *New Light on Martin Luther*.

Here follows a short paragraph on p. 163 of the biography: "In his very lucid and penetrating book Erasmus said that the controversy had recently been renewed by Carlstadt and by Eck, 'but in a moderate way.' After that Luther took it up 'more violently.' Now the author devotes a book of his own to it, 'urged on by his friends.' People will shout, he says, that the world is turned upside down. Erasmus dares to withstand Luther. That is like a mouse fighting against an elephant. Nevertheless, it has to be done. He has never accepted Luther's doctrines and he simply must state his own position. Luther should not be scandalized to note that Erasmus disagrees with him, since Luther has already disagreed with all the doctors of the Church, all the schools, all the councils, all the popes."

The present writer in his article in the *Archiv für Reformationsgeschichte* supported the verdict by A. Renaudet, who stated that it was Luther who "sent Erasmus back to Rome in 1525 with his violent blast in the form of his famous book, *De servo arbitrio.*" The writer on p. 164 drew this conclusion: "Having joined the ranks of those whom he had often savagely attacked, the great humanist was obliged to restate his position, particularly on the seventh sacrament. He now ceased to deprecate celibacy and moderate asceticism." More than ten years have passed since the two statements mentioned above were published by the present writer. He now believes that the problem was more complicated than Renaudet and he thought. As we study once more the declaration made by Erasmus on September 6, 1524, we must draw the conclusion that Erasmus himself precipitated the breach between himself and Luther. The latter could not very well ignore the bitter remarks by his present adversary. For the latter claimed that he had disagreed with "all the doctors of the Church, all the schools, all the councils, all the popes." After that blast Luther was forced to break completely with his former protector.

Now we are faced with an intriguing problem. Just why did those two powerful men have to cause the awful chasm between Roman Catholicism and Protestantism? For that is exactly what they did in September 1524. Melanchthon obviously understood exactly what Erasmus had done. In many earlier literary productions he had stated that Luther had an admirable insight into the Gospel of Christ. For three years in a row, as Duke George of Saxony had said, he had refused to side against Luther. For that reason he had been forced to leave Louvain, where he had had some bitter enemies. But after September 6, 1524, he was in a good position to go back to Louvain. Now he had enemies everywhere, even in Basel. He finally had to flee from Basel to Freiburg, though later on he once more returned to Basel. It seems strange that his native country now could not reclaim him.

What we must do at this stage is to study carefully the whole letter addressed to Melanchthon and Duke George of Saxony. Erasmus argued first about his work at the University of Louvain. There he had made some powerful enemies, who claimed that he had been "in league with Luther." Then his friends, noting that he was in danger of being hurt by his attempts to shield Luther, "held out the hope to the Pope and the princes that I would publish something against Luther." Erasmus himself also "cherished the same hope." But when he observed that his so-called friends began to assail him with books, there was nothing else left for him to do except to publish what he had already written before. For otherwise he would have "made enemies of the rulers." To the latter he had given his word to go ahead and try to check Luther in his reckless behavior from 1521 to 1524. Next there came Luther's letter in which he promised not to attack Erasmus on condition that the latter "would keep silent." Finally "the rabid evangelicals would have been more bitter against me than they are, for I handled the subject very moderately." He had written nothing except what he actually believed. He was now willing to desist if he should become convinced that it were better to do so rather than go ahead and make matters still worse.

On the other hand, his moderate friends feared that he was "putting it into the hands of the tyrants to use cruelty." But he replied that no one ever discouraged cruelty more than he himself had done. Even if he were "heart and soul with the papal party," he should still "have persuaded them from cruelty, for that is the way the evil is spread." For example, "the theologians believed that if they burned one or two men in Brussels, everybody would change his way of thinking." However, "the death of those men made many Lutherans." That was perfectly true. At the same time it became clear to Erasmus that the so-called evangelicals were all wrong in concluding that the "Gospel would go to ruin if anybody opposed their madness." The Gospel was not given unto the human race that anybody could "sin with impunity."

The message to Duke George stated that there were two reasons why Erasmus had not yet obeyed the exhortations to side against Luther. In the first place, his age and temperament made it unwise for him to enter a ferocious battle. In the second place, he thought that Luther and his doctrine were in a sense "a sort of necessary evil in the corrupt state of the Church." Although the "medicine was somewhat bitter, and also violent, he hoped that "it would produce some health in the body of the people of Christ." Unfortunately, many people interpreted his moderation as collusion with Luther, which was not the case at all. Moreover, "under the cover of the Gospel a new people is growing up, which is wordy, shameless, and intractable – exactly the kind that Luther himself cannot endure." Nevertheless they "revile Luther himself as much as they despise the bishops and princes." King Henry VIII of England and Pope Clement VII have given Erasmus "the spur in their letters." But strange though it may seem, he did not react to those messages as much as to "audacity of some of those brawlers who will destroy both the Gospel and literature unless they are put down." He had hoped that "the tyranny of the Pharisees might be done away with, not merely changed." However, if it must be kept, he would "prefer popes and bishops to those low Phalarides, who are more intolerable than all the rest."

In the book itself Erasmus argues as follows: He and Luther both have little respect for medieval civilization, and for that reason they prefer to consult the works of the Church Fathers, most of whose productions Erasmus himself published. One reason why he had moved from Louvain to Basel was to be near his chief publisher, in whose home he resided for the first ten months. That was Froben, but we must not overlook the fact that his edition of the New Testament was issued by seven publishers in Basel alone. His *Praise of Folly* was published in nine different cities! In Cologne and Venice he had three publishers. Nevertheless, he favored Froben above all the others. Louvain was not a great center of printing, and on the local campus classical antiquity was not so highly regarded as it was in Basel. The big issue was this: How great was the authority of the Bible? A book inspired by the Holy Spirit should bear more weight than all other sources. Very true, but the Holy Spirit has not ceased His operations. To whom has the power of inspiration passed? Probably to those worthy souls who seek to imitate Jesus Christ. Each Christian must be very careful not to interpret the Bible recklessly.

There are texts in the Bible that strongly favor the doctrine of free will, while others are very different. There are two extremes opposed to each other. Both came from the Holy Spirit. Man is finite and does not understand this situation. He must seek to reconcile the two opposite views. It seems that nobody can make a contribution to his own salvation, and yet he must have some responsibility. God does not force any human being into damnation. If God compels man to do good works, He must also be responsible for the sins committed by man. Here Erasmus in 1524 entered upon a dangerous path. He was unable to understand that God could cause good works and would refuse to cause evil works. Satan was in charge of the latter department. Gerard Groote and Gerard Zerbolt had stated clearly that man has no power of his own with which to aid in the process of salvation. Erasmus was moving away from the spirit of the Devotio Moderna. It would have been better for him to have remained in the Low Countries.

Groote wrote as follows: "God is the 'summum bonum;' if we have him, we have all goodness; if we lose him, nothing but evil is left unto us." He goes on to indicate that the part of us which is divine cannot exist without the life-giving contact with Him who alone can sustain life and nourish our inner selves. Even Jesus Christ in referring to His humanity said: "I of myself can do nothing." And yet Erasmus was correct in arguing that man must have some responsibility. He says that if human beings were unable to heed God's warnings, why should God have issued them? Moreover, Luther's reply was not to his credit. The present writer in his biography of Luther has quoted more than two pages in fine print (166-168). His opinion is that here Luther missed a wonderful opportunity to heal the breach between himself and his opponents.

Of great importance also is the letter which Erasmus on December 12, 1524, addressed to Duke George of Saxony. The present writer has devoted pp. 259-264 to this epistle. On p. 260 we find some interesting information about a publisher of his in Louvain: "I found, while I was living in Brabant, that Froben, at the instigation of certain scholars, Capito among them had printed certain books of Luther's. I wrote him a letter telling him he could not retain my friendship if he continued to defile his press with such books. Not content with this, I added a note to my book on Colloquies, which was then in press at Louvain, in which I clearly testified that I was altogether out of sympathy with the Lutheran party." On p. 262 we find an illuminating reference to the theme of disintegration since the Apostolic Age: "I often sigh to myself when I consider to what depths Christian piety has fallen. The world had been numbed by ceremonies, bad monks reigned unpunished and had caught men's consciences in snares that could not be loosed." So the thought came to him that perhaps the diseases of his age required a remedy like that which Luther seemed to prescribe. And on p. 264 we read this: "Luther has offered the world a violent and bitter medicine. Whatever the remedy, I have wished that the body of the Church, everywhere corrupted by so many ills, might gain some health."

After the year 1524 came eleven years of upheavals, persecution, bitter quarrels among the highest authorities, scandals in the Papal Court, and wild disorders by certain Anabaptists and other Protestants. Gradually Erasmus became more and more disappointed by both Roman Catholic and Protestant leaders. He studied with great care the benefits of celibacy, the message by Christ about that subject in Matthew XIX, and the exhortations issued still by the Brethren and Sisters of the Common Life. In his *Catechism* he summed up his own philosophy of life. It was dedicated to the father of Anna Boleyn, the second wife of Henry VIII.

It may seem remarkable that Erasmus would favor a man whose daughter had replaced Catherine of Aragon, the first wife of King Henry VIII. But then we must always bear in mind that he remained as before the close friend of the king. We saw above that he received upon the accession of Henry VIII a letter written "in his own hand." No wonder that after this evidence of affection and admiration on the part of the powerful monarch he continued to support him to the best of his ability. In the famous edition of Erasmus' *Opera* published from 1703 to 1706 and reprinted in 1961, we find on columns 1133-1134 of Vol. V the following dedication: "Clarissimo Viro D. Thomas A. Roscheford, Comiti Ormoniae et Wilscheriae." The date is given as M.D. XXXIII. In the first sentence of the text Erasmus says that he will discuss the faith of the Catholic Church, "outside of which there can be no salvation."

As we have just seen, the treatise was dedicated to Viscount Rochford, the father of Anne Boleyn, who later became the mother of Queen Elizabeth. Little did Erasmus know in 1533 about the latter's hatred of the Roman Catholics. He was now living in Freiburg im Breisgau, because the majority of the citizens of Basel were Protestants or at least hostile to the Roman Catholic authorities. He started this composition as follows: "A short time ago the thought occurred to me to write something in fellowship with the Catholic Church. It is the House of God, outside of which there can be no salvation."[1]

It seems incredible that the notorious Index of 1559 condemned all the writings of Erasmus, including the extremely pro-Catholic work entitled, *Catechismus*. The Roman Catholic authorities certainly were poorly informed about this particular book, as well as about several others. There the author assailed the Lutherans and praised the staunch defenders of the Roman Catholic Church. Even today there are some historians who write as follows about Queen Elizabeth: "The Elizabethan settlement breathed the spirit of the Erasmian attempt to achieve comprehension through minimal doctrinal demands."

---

[1] D. Erasmus, *Symbolum sive Catechismus*, L. B. edition, Vol. V, col. 1133: "Jam dudum mihi gestit animus adscribi in consortium Ecclesiae Catholica, quae est domus Dei, extra quam nulli speranda salus externa."

CHAPTER XIV

The Colloquies

The most highly controversial book written by Erasmus was the collection of conversations, mostly in the form of dialogues, known as *The Colloquies*. We fortunately have now at our disposal a magnificent volume which contains all the editions of importance in English translation. It was published in 1965 by the University of Chicago Press and edited by Craig R. Thompson. The only complaint about the numerous comments made by him which the present writer has published in his essay on Erasmus for the collection issued in November 1969 by the University of Louvain is to the effect that Thompson disapproved of the condemnation issued by the Sorbonne in 1526 of some of his conversations. The writer also was displeased with Erasmus for having slandered the reputation of John Standonck, in whose dormitory Erasmus spent his first year as a student at the University of Paris.

We shall start with the scandalous colloquy which describes conditions there in the year 1495. Erasmus writes as follows: "That college was then ruled by Jean Standonck, a man whose intentions were beyond reproach but whom you have found entirely lacking in judgment . . . Within a year he had succeeded in killing many very capable, gifted, promising students; and others, some of whom I knew, he reduced to blindness, breakdowns, or leprosy. Not a single student was safe."

These witty comments remind us of a naughty report by Erasmus addressed in 1497 to an English student in Paris named Thomas Grey, who was being tutored by the ambitious young humanist. We have quoted it above: "I have amused myself in making fun of some pseudo-theologians of our time, whose brains are rotten, their language barbarous, their intellects dull, their learning a bed of thorns, their intellects dull, their learning a bed of thorns . . . and their hearts as black as ink." He was clearly referring to the scholastic philosophers and theologians

---

[1] D. Erasmus, *Colloquies*, ed. C. R. Thompson, p. 352.

at the Sorbonne, the theological faculty in the University of Paris. Moreover, in 1497 he also issued the first edition of a sarcastic work called *Ratio Studii*, or *De Ratione Studii*. Here he did not yet include references to Christian literature but chiefly to Lucian, Demosthenes, Herodotus, Aristophanes, Homer, Euripides, Terence, Plautus, Virgil, Horace, Cicero, Caesar, and Sallust. Among the pagan philosophers he referred with great respect to Plato, Aristotle, Theophrastus, Plotinus, Pliny, Macrobius, and Aulus Gellius. But in the later editions he mentioned St. Augustine, Jerome, Origen, Chrysostom, Ambrose, and Basil. In all the versions he showed little respect for the scholastic philosophers and theologians.[1]

Thompson informs us that the colloquy from which we have just quoted was the longest of all, and it was first "printed in the edition of February, 1526." Consequently, when we study the statement to the effect that one speaker had lived in Standonck's dormitory "thirty years ago," we are aware of the fact that Erasmus was indirectly talking about his own experiences there. He spent most of his time from 1522 to 1529 in Basel, where he lived among German-speaking citizens, in an atmosphere very different from that in Louvain. He left the latter city in November 1521, chiefly because he could no longer sympathize with his colleagues at the local university, though certainly not because he did not like their pro-Catholic attitude. It is worth noting here that as soon as the majority of Basel's inhabitants became Protestants in the year 1529, he moved to Freiburg im Breisgau. And when he died in Basel during the year 1536, he was not by any means there to stay longer than he had to in order to supervise the publication of his pro-Catholic works.

Now we must examine a colloquy which caused great animosity at the Sorbonne in the year 1523. It was entitled, "The Repentant Girl." Thompson says this in his introduction: "To the Sorbonne's complaint that the youth commends the girl for not staying in the convent, Erasmus retorted that what Eubulus really congratulates her upon is her promptness in leaving after she had decided she could not stay and before she had made profession . . . It is not likely that this distinction appeased his critics." Thompson was correct in his deduction. Eubulus asks Catherine who "those birds" are. He says this about the prior of the convent: "He's prior of the community. Don't steal away

---

[1] See the reprint of the article published by the writer in *Archiv für Reformationsgeschichte* (1957) in *The Youth of Erasmus* (1968, p. 374).

— they've been boozing a long time already." Then Eubulus asks Catherine how she overcame the opposition of her parents. She replies as follows: "First, by the shameless insistence of the monks and nuns." This reminds us of the reply Erasmus gave to Servatius, the prior at Steyn who in the year 1514 ordered him to return. He replied that he would not go back to the customary "drinking parties." Very interesting is the following observation by Eubulus: "Those women had put a spell on you, or rather had charmed your wits away. But you stuck to your decision all the while?"[1]

Thompson in his introduction correctly makes much of the fact that Nicholas Baechem, prior of the Carmelites at Louvain, as early as 1522 wanted to burn the *Colloquies*, "in which he thought he detected Lutheran heresies."[2] It is illuminating in this connection that Erasmus in the second version of his *Book Against the Barbarians* condemned the following three monastic orders: Franciscans (*Minorita*), Dominicans (called here *Jacobita*, as happened in some areas), and Carmelites."[3] No doubt Baechem's animosity in Louvain had been noted by the author before he published this second version in the year 1520. And again, this animosity was one of the reasons why Erasmus finally moved from Louvain to Basel. Thompson also informs us about the attitude displayed by the Sorbonne in the year 1526. In May 1526, so he reports, "the faculty, in a petition to the Parlement, formally censured the *Colloquies* (along with passages from other writings by Erasmus), denouncing sixty-nine passages as 'erroneous, scandalous, or impious' and describing their author as 'a pagan who mocks at the Christian religion and its sacred rites and customs.'" The book should be forbidden to all, especially to young persons. Thompson continues as follows: "When rumors of the Sorbonne's deliberations of May, 1526, reached him, Erasmus added to the June, 1526 edition of the *Colloquies* a letter to the reader in defense of his book." This letter was entitled, *De Utilitate Colloquiorum*, from which we quote a few sentences below, as published by Thompson:

"Now, since in addition to dealing with refinement of language I have

[1] D. Erasmus, *Colloquies*, Thompson ed., pp. 112-113. Next we note that Catherine became stubborn: "Certainly, for they said this happens to many who vow themselves to Christ."
[2] D. Erasmus, *Colloquies*, ed. C. R. Thompson, p. xxx.
[3] A. Hyma, *The Youth of Erasmus*, second ed. p. 262: "Quid enim aliud fit cum Minorita, aut Jacobita, aut Carmelita, velut oraculum consulitur, cui puer ad optimas disciplinas destinatus, formandus tradi debeat, quibus rationibus et autoribus instituendus sit, non aliter quam Demodocus ille Platonicus consulebat Socratem."

added here and there some passages to direct the mind toward religion, they slander me; and they probe the syllables through and through, precisely as if the dogmas of the Christian creed were solemnly spelled out in these pages! How mischievously they do this will be plainer when I have demonstrated the uncommon utility of the *Colloquies.*" First he takes up pilgrimages to places far away from home: "Hither, over such vast stretches of land and sea, hasten venerable bishops, deserting the flocks committed to their care; hither princes, their house and realm abandoned; hither husbands, their wives and children – of whose conduct and virtue the husband is necessarily guardian – left at home; hither young men and women, not without grave risk to morals and chastity." Under the next topic he takes up the "pursuit of benefices," in which many ambitious persons lose "morals and money both." Then follows a discussion of a soldier's confession, to which one colloquy was devoted. And in *The Master's Bidding* he says he teaches "a boy modesty and manners suitable to his age." Similarly, "In *Youthful Piety,* do I not inspire the young mind by means of godly precepts, with a zeal for righteousness? The carping by some persons at the part on confession was sheer slander, to which I replied long ago." In this manner he discusses a large number of colloquies, in order to refute his critics.[1]

In the year 1528 the Sorbonne was supported by the faculties of law and medicine, and here Thompson argues that Erasmus did not lose his head, because of pride on his part.[2] Nevertheless, there was very little cause for pride when these three faculties in Europe's greatest university and city hurled bitter accusations against him. He had sided with immoral writers of all ages in publishing tales and conversations under the following titles: "Courtship," "The Reptentant Girl," "Marriage," "The Young Man and the Harlot," and "A Marriage in Name Only." Thompson, the editor, states on p. 99 that "at the least we shall understand better why he and his *Colloquies* seemed a scandal to the orthodox." One was entitled, "The Epicurean." Thompson did not realize that Erasmus in the Year 1533 experienced a genuine conversion, to which we shall devote a whole chapter. He now supported the view of Jesus Christ on the subject of chastity, which differed a great deal from that of the Apostle Paul as far as married life was concerned.

We are reproducing below two popular *Colloquies,* which had been published by the present writer in the year 1930 as a part of a source entitled, *Erasmus and the Humanists* (New York: Crofts).

[1] D. Erasmus, *Colloquies,* ed. C. R. Thompson, pp. 624-637.
[2] *Ibidem,* pp. 624.

THE SOURCES

PART III. THE COLLOQUIES

10. *A Dialogue by Anthony and Adolph.* [Erasmus, *Opera*, Leyden ed., I, 712-715.]

THE SHIPWRECK

A.[1] This is a dreadful story that you are telling. Is that sailing? God forbid that any such idea should come into my head.

B.[2] Indeed, what I have related is mere child's play compared with what you are about to hear.

A. I have heard more than enough of mishaps. I shudder while you narrate them, as though I myself were present at the danger.

B. Indeed, to me past struggles are pleasing. That night something happened which almost put the captain at his wits' end.

A. What I pray?

B. The moon was bright that night, and one of the sailors was standing in the topmast (for so it is called, I believe), keeping a lookout for land. A globe of fire appeared beside him. It is considered by sailors to be an evil omen if the fire be single, a good omen if it be double. In ancient times these were thought to be Castor and Pollux.

A. What have they to do with sailors? One of them was a horseman, the other a boxer.

B. Well, this is the view of the poets. The captain who was sitting at the helm began to speak. "Mate", said he (for sailors address each other in this manner), "do you see what is beside you?" "I see", he replied, "and I hope it may be lucky." Soon the fiery globe descended along the rigging and rolled to the captain.

A. Was he paralyzed with fear?

B. Sailors are accustomed to strange sights. The globe stopped there a while, then rolled along the side of the vessel and disappeared down through the middle of the deck. About noon the storm began to rage with great fury. Have you ever seen the Alps?

A. Yes, I have.

B. Those mountains are warts compared with the waves of the sea.

---

[1] A. stands for Anthony.
[2] B. stands for Adolph.

When we were lifted up on the crest of a wave, we might have touched the moon with our fingers. As often as we went down between the billows, we seemed to be going directly to the infernal regions, the earth opening to receive us.

A. Madmen to trust themselves to the sea!

B. The sailors struggled in vain against the tempest, and at length the captain, quite pale, came toward us.

A. That pallor presages some great evil.

B. "Friends," says he, "I have lost control of my ship. The winds have conquered me, and nothing remains but to put our trust in God, and to prepare for the end."

A. A truly Scythian speech!

B. "But first," says he, "we shall relieve the ship of her cargo. Necessity, a stern mistress, commands this. It is better to save our lives, with the loss of our goods, than to perish along with our goods." The truth of this was evident to us; and many boxes of precious goods were thrown into the sea.

A. This was indeed a loss!

B. There was a certain Italian who had been upon an embassy to the king of Scotland; he had a box full of silver and gold, plates, rings, cloth, and silk garments.

A. Would he not settle with the sea?

B. No; he wished either to perish with his beloved wealth, or to be saved along with it; and so he refused.

A. What did the captain say?

B. "So far as we are concerned," says he, "you are welcome to perish with your goods; but it is not right that we should all be endangered for the sake of your box, and rather than that we will throw you headlong into the sea, along with your box."

A. A speech worthy of a sailor.

B. So the Italian also threw over his goods, with many an oath, regretting that he had trusted his life to so barbarous an element. A little later the winds, in no wise softened by our offerings, broke the rigging and tore the sails into shreds.

A. Too bad! Too bad!

B. Again the skipper approaches us.

A. With further information?

B. He greets us: "Friends, the time has come that everybody should commend himself to God and prepare for death." When some of the passengers who had some knowledge of the sea asked him how many hours he thought he could keep afloat, he said he could not say for certain, but that it would not be above three hours.

A. This news was more serious than the former.

B. With these words he ordered all ropes to be severed and the mast cut with a saw close to the deck, and to be thrown into the sea together with the spars.

A. Why?

B. Because the sails, being torn to pieces, were a burden rather than a help. All our hope was in the helm.

A. What were the passengers doing in the meantime?

B. There you might have seen a wretched spectacle. The sailors, singing "SALVE, REGINA," implored the Virgin Mother, calling her star of the sea, queen of heaven, ruler of the world, harbor of safety, and flattering her with many other titles, which the Bible nowhere attributes to her.

A. What has she to do with the sea, who never sailed, so far as I know?

B. Venus formerly had the care of sailors, because she was supposed to have been born of the sea. Since she has ceased to care for them, the Virgin Mother has been substituted for her: as a mother and not as a virgin.

A. You are joking.

B. Some fell down upon the decks and worshipped the sea, pouring oil upon the waves, flattering them as we used to flatter an angry prince.

A. What did they say?

B. "O most merciful sea! O most generous sea! O most wealthy sea! Have pity, save us!" Many things of this sort they sang to the deaf sea.

A. Ridiculous superstition! What were the others doing?

B. Some were occupied with sea-sickness; but most of them offered vows. Among them was a certain Englishman, who promised mountains of gold to our Lady of Walsingham, if only he might reach land alive. Some promised much to the wood of the cross in a certain place; others to the same wood in another place. The same was done for the Virgin Mary, who reigns in many places; and they think the vow is of no avail, unless one names the place.

A. Absurd! As if the saints did not dwell in heaven.

B. Some vowed to be Carthusians. One promised to go to James of Compostella with bare head and feet, his body covered only with an iron coat of mail, and begging his food.

A. Did nobody mention Christopher?

B. I could not help laughing when I heard one with a loud voice (lest he should not be heard) promise Chrisopher in the high church at Paris, a mountain rather than a statue, a wax candle as big as he himself. While he was shouting this at the top of his voice, with now and then an additional emphasis, an acquaintance nudged him with his elbow and said, "Take care what you promise; for if you sell all your goods at auction, you will not be able to pay." Then said he in a lower voice, lest Christopher should hear: "Hold your tongue, fool; do you think I am in earnest? When once I reach land, I will not give him a tallow candle."

A. What a blockhead! I imagine he was a Hollander.

B. No, but he was a Zeelander.[1]

A. I am surprised that nobody thought of Paul the Apostle. He himself sailed, and when the ship was wrecked, leaped ashore; and he learned through misfortune to succor the unfortunate.

B. There was no mention of Paul.

A. Did they pray meanwhile?

B. Earnestly. One sang "SALVE, REGINA," another the apostles' creed. Some had special prayers, like charms, against danger.

A. How religious men are in times of affliction! In prosperity neither God nor saint comes into our head. What were you doing all this time? Did you offer vows to none of the saints?

B. Not one.

A. Why not?

B. Because I do not bargain with the saints. For what else is it than a contract: "I will give this if you will do that; I will give you a wax candle, if I swim out of this; I will go to Rome, if you will save me."

A. But did you not implore the protection of some saint?

B. Not even that.

A. Why not?

B. Because Heaven is a large place. If I commend myself to some saint, St. Peter for example, who is most likely to hear me first of all, since he stands at the door; before he goes to God and explains my case I should have perished.

A. What did you do, then?

B. I went straight to the Father himself, saying: "Our Father who art in heaven." None of the saints hears sooner than He, nor gives more willingly what is asked.

---

[1] Zeeland and Holland were Dutch counties.

A. But in the meanwhile did not your conscience cry out against you? Were you not afraid to call him Father whom you have offended with so many transgressions?

B. To tell the truth, my conscience did terrify me a little; but presently I gathered courage, thinking, there is no father so angry with his son, but, if he sees him in danger, in a river or a lake, would seize him by the hair and draw him out upon the bank. Among them all no one behaved more quietly than a certain woman who had a baby in her arms, which she was nursing.

A. What did she do?

B. She was the only one who did not shout or weep or promise. Embracing her child, she prayed silently. In the meantime the ship was struck by a big wave, and the captain, fearing lest it should go to pieces, bound it fore and aft with cables.

A. What a miserable makeshift!

B. Then an aged priest, sixty years old, whose name was Adam, comes forward. Casting off his clothes even to his shirt and his leather stockings he ordered that we should prepare ourselves in a similar manner for swimming; and standing thus in the middle of the ship he preached to us out of Gerson the five truths concerning the usefulness of confession, exhorting us all to prepare ourselves for life or death. There was also a Dominican to whom those who wished confessed.

A. What did you do?

B. Seeing that confusion reigned everywhere, I confessed silently to God, condemning my unrighteousness and imploring his mercy.

A. Where would you have gone, if you had died thus?

B. I left that to God as judge; nor was I disposed to be my own judge; yet in the meantime I was not without some hope. While these things were going on, the sailor returns to us weeping. "Let every one prepare himself," says he, "for the ship will not last a quarter of an hour." For it was badly broken, and the sea was rushing in. A little later the sailor informed us that he saw a church tower, and advised us to pray to the saint for aid, whoever might be the patron of that church. All fall upon their knees and pray to the unknown saint.

A. If you had called him by name perhaps he might have heard you.

B. He was unknown to us. Meanwhile the captain steers the ship, shattered as it was, and leaking at every seam, and evidently ready to fall to pieces, had it not been bound with cables.

A. A sad condition of affairs.

B. We came so near the shore that the inhabitants of the place saw our danger; and running in crowds to the beach, they held up their coats and put their hats upon lances, to attract our attention; and they raised their arms, to show that they were sorry for us.

A. I am anxious to know what happened.

B. The sea had already invaded the whole ship, so that we were likely to be no safer in the ship than in the sea.

A. Then you were obliged to flee to the holy anchor?

B. Nay, to the miserable one. The sailors bail out the boat and lower it into the sea. All attempt to crowd into it, and the sailors remonstrate vigorously, saying that the boat is not able to hold such a crowd; that each one should lay hold of whatever he could find and take to swimming. There was no opportunity for deliberation. One took an oar, another a boat-hook, another a tub, another a plank; and all took to the waves, each one resting upon his means of salvation.

A. In the meantime what became of that poor woman who alone did not cry out?

B. She reached land first.

A. How was that possible?

B. We placed her upon a wide board, and tied her on it so that she could not very well fall off. We gave her a paddle in her hand which she might use instead of an oar, and, wishing her well, we set her adrift, pushing her forward with a pole, so that she might float wide of the ship, from which there was danger. She held her baby with her left hand and paddled with her right.

A. What a courageous woman!

B. When nothing was left, some one pulled down a wooden image of the Virgin Mother, now rotten and hollowed out by the rats, and embracing it, began to swim.

A. Did the boat arrive safe?

B. They were the first ones to be lost.

A. How did that happen?

B. Before it could get clear of the ship it tipped and was overturned.

A. How badly managed! What then?

B. While watching the others I nearly perished myself.

A. How so?

B. Because nothing remained for me to swim upon.

A. Corks would have been of use there.

B. Just at this time I would rather have had some cheap cork than a golden candlestick. Finally, as I was looking about, it occurred to me that the stump of the mast would be of use to me; but as I could not get it out alone, I got a companion to help me. We both threw ourselves upon it and so committed ourselves to the sea, I upon the right end, he upon the left. While we were thus tossing about, the sea chaplain threw himself upon the middle, between our shoulders. He was a stout man. We cried out: "Who is this third man? He will cause us all to perish!" He, on the other hand, mildly replied: "Be of good cheer; there is room enough. God will be with us."

A. Why did he come so late?

B. He was to have been in the boat with the Dominican, for they all had great respect for him; but although they had confessed to one another on the ship, they had forgotten something (I know not what), wherefore they began confessing again at the ship's rail, and one laid his hand upon the other. Meanwhile the boat is turned over, as Adam himself told me.

A. What became of the Dominican?

B. He, the same one told me, implored the saints' help, put off his clothes and took to swimming all naked.

A. What saints did he invoke?

B. Dominic, Thomas, Vincent; but he relied most upon Catherine of Sens.

A. Did he say nothing of Christ?

B. Not a word, according to the priest.

A. He would have done better if he had not put off his holy cowl; with that off, how could Catherine of Sens recognize him? But go on about yourself.

B. While we were tossing about near the ship, which rolled hither and thither at the mercy of the waves, the helm broke the thigh of the man who held the left end of our float, and he was knocked off. The priest prayed for his eternal rest, and succeeded to his place, urging me to hold courageously to my end and move my feet actively. In the meanwhile we swallowed a great deal of salt water. Neptune had mixed for us not only a salt bath, but a salt drink. The priest, however, soon had a remedy for that.

A. What, I pray?

B. Every time a wave came toward us, he turned the back of his head to it with his mouth firmly closed.

A. You say he was a stout old man?

B. Swimming thus for some time we had made considerable progress when the priest, who was a man of unusual height, said: "Be of good cheer; I feel bottom." Not having dared to hope for such happiness, I replied: "We are yet too far from shore to hope to find bottom."

"No," he said, "I feel the ground with my feet." "It is," I rejoined, "some of the boxes, perhaps, which the sea has thrown down here." "No," said he, "I plainly feel the earth by scratching with my toes." We swam on for some time longer, and he felt bottom again. "You must do," he said, "what you think is best. I will give you the whole mast and trust myself to the bottom"; and at the same time waiting for the waves to flow outward, he went forward as rapidly as he could. When the waves came again upon him, holding firmly to his knees with both hands he met the wave, sinking beneath it as sea-gulls and ducks are accustomed to do; and when the wave again receded he sprang up and ran. Seeing that this succeeded in his case, I did the same. Then some of the strongest of those who stood upon the beach, and those most used to the waves, fortified themselves against the force of the waves with long poles stretched between them, so that the outermost held out a pole to the swimmer; and when he had grasped it, the whole line moved shorewards and so he was drawn safely on dry land. Some were saved in this way.

A. How many?

B. Seven; but of these, two fainted with the heat, when placed before the fire.

A. How many were there in the ship?

A. Fifty-eight.

A. O cruel sea! At least it might have been content with the tithes, which suffice for the priests. Did it return so few out of so great a number?

B. We were surprisingly well treated by the people, who most cheerfully furnished us with everything, lodging, fire, food, clothes, and provisions for our homeward journey.

A. What people were they?

B. Hollanders.

A. No people are more civil, although they are surrounded with savage nations. You will not go to sea again, I take it?

B. Not if God keeps my mind sound.

A. And as for me, I would rather hear such tales than experience them.

11. *A Dialoque between Robert and William.* [Erasmus, *Opera*, Leyden ed., 1, 715-718.]

THE INNS

A.[1] Why do so many people stop at Lyons for two or three days? As for me, when I start upon a journey I do not rest until I reach my destination.

B.[2] Indeed, I wonder how any one can be got away from the place at all.

A. Why?

B. Because that is the place from which the companions of Ulysses could not have been drawn. The Sirens are there. No one is treated better in his own home than there at an inn.

A. What do they do?

B. The women are very handsome there, and one of them is always standing near the table to divert the guests with wit and fun. First the mistress of the house came to us, and bade us welcome. Then came the daughter, a fine woman, merry and charming, so that she might have amused Cato himself. Nor do they talk to their guests as if they were strangers, but as if they were old acquaintances.

A. Yes, I admit that French people are very civil.

B. But since they could not be present all the time (the business of the house had to be attended to and the other guests had to be greeted), a girl well supplied with jokes attended us during the whole meal. She was quite able to repay all the jesters in their own coin. She kept the stories going until the daughter returned. The mother, by the way, was somewhat elderly.

A. But what sort of fare did you have with all this? For the stomach is not filled with stories.

B. Fine! Indeed, I wonder how they can entertain guests so cheaply. Then too, after dinner they divert the guests with pleasant conversation, lest they should feel bored. It seemed to me that I was at home, not travelling.

A. How about the sleeping accommodations?

B. Even there we were attended by girls, laughing, romping and playing; they asked us if we had any soiled clothes, washed them for us and brought them back. What more can I say? We saw nothing but

---

[1] A. stands for Robert.   [2] B. stands for William.

women and girls, except in the stables; and even there they burst in occasionally. They treat departing guests as affectionately as if they were all brothers or near relatives.

A. Very likely such manners suit the French; as for me, the customs of Germany please me more. They are more manly.

B. I never happened to visit Germany; so tell me how the Germans entertain a guest.

A. I cannot say what happens in all parts of Germany, but I will relate what I have seen. Upon the arrival of the guest nobody greets him, lest they should seem to court him for they consider that mean and unworthy of German dignity and gravity. When you have shouted yourself hoarse, finally someone puts his head out of the window of the stove-room (for they live there up to the middle of the summer), just as a snail pokes its head out of its shell. You have to ask him if you may be entertained there. If he says nothing, you understand that room will be made for you. To your inquiries, with a wave of his hand, he indicates where the stables are. There you are permitted to take care of your horse as you choose; for no servant lifts a finger. If the tavern is a large one, a servant will show you the stables and a rather inconvenient place for your horse. They keep the better places for the noblemen, who, as they pretend, are expected. If you find fault with anything, you are told at once that you are at liberty to hunt another tavern. In the cities it is difficult to get any hay, even a little, and it is almost as dear as oats. When your horse is provided for, you go just as you are to the stove-room, boots, baggage and mud. There is one room for all comers.

B. Among the French they take the guests to bed rooms, where they may change their clothes, bathe and warm themselves, or even take a nap, if they please.

A. Well, there is no such thing here. In the stove-room you take off your boots and put on slippers. If you like, you change your shirt; you hang your clothes, wet with rain, against the stove; and you sit by it yourself, in order to get dry. There is water ready if you care to wash your hands, but it is generally so dirty that you have to seek more water to wash off that ablution.

B. I cannot admire such manly people.

A. Even if you arrive at four in the afternoon, you cannot get your supper before nine, and sometimes ten.

B. Why is that?

A. They serve nothing until they see all the guests assembled, in order that the same effort may serve for all.

B. They have an eye to labor-saving.

A. You are right. And thus very often between eighty and a hundred persons are assembled in the same stoveroom, footmen, horsemen, tradesmen, sailors, coachmen, farmers, boys, women, healthy people and sick people.

B. That is in truth a community.

A. One is combing his head, another wiping the perspiration from his face, another cleaning his winter shoes or boots, another reeks of garlic. What more could you desire? Here is no less confusion of tongue and of persons than there was once in the tower of Babel. But if they see a foreigner who shows some evidence of distinction in dress, they are all interested in him, and stare at him as if he were some animal from Africa. Even after they are at the table, they turn their heads to get a look, and neglect their meals rather than lose sight of him.

B. At Rome, Paris, and Venice there is no such gazing.

A. Remember, it is a mortal sin to call for anything. When the evening is far advanced and no more guests are expected, an old servant appears, with gray beard, cropped head, a savage look and shabby clothes.

B. It was necessary that such should be cup-bearers to the Roman Cardinals . . .

A. Well, after all are seated, the grim servant comes out and counts his company. By and by he returns and sets before each guest a wooden dish and a spoon of the same kind of silver; then a glass and a little piece of bread. Each one polishes up his utensils in a leisurely way while the porridge is cooking. And thus they sit not uncommonly for upwards of an hour.

B. Does no guest call for food in the meantime?

A. No one who is acquainted with the temper of the country. At length wine is served, and wine that is far from being tasteless! Those who water their wine ought to drink no other kind, it is so thin and sharp. But if any guest wants better wine, offering to pay extra for it, they will give him a look as if they wished to murder him. If he insists upon it they answer that a great many counts and margraves have lodged there and none of them has complained of the quality of the wine; if it does not suit him, why then, let him go to another tavern, for they look upon their noblemen as the only men of importance, and exhibit their coats of arms everywhere. By this time the guests get a crust to throw to their barking stomachs. By and by the dishes come on in great array. The first usually consists of pieces of bread soaked in meat-broth, or, if it be fish-day, in a broth of herbs. After this comes another kind of broth, then some kind of warmed-up meat or salt fish. Again the porridge is brought on, then some more substantial food, until, when the stomach is well tamed, they serve up roast meat or boiled fish, which is not to be despised. But here they are sparing, and take the dishes away quickly. In this way they diversify the entertainment, like comedians who mix choruses with their scenes, taking care that the last act shall be the best.

B. This is indeed the mark of a good poet.

A. Moreover, it would be an unpardonable offense if anybody in the meantime should say: "Take away this dish; nobody cares for it." You must sit there through the prescribed time, which they measure, I suppose, with an hourglass. At last, the bearded fellow, or the innkeeper himself, who wears no better clothes than the servants, comes in and asks if there is anything wanted. Presently some better wine is brought in. They admire him the most who drinks the most; but although he is the greater consumer he pays no more than he who drinks least.

B. A curious people, indeed!

A. The result is that sometimes there are those who consume twice the value in wine of what they pay for the whole meal. But before I end my account of this entertainment, it is wonderful what a noise and confusion of voices arises, when all have begun to grow warm with drink. It is unnecessary to say that the riot is universal. So-called jesters thrust themselves in everywhere, and although there is no kind of human beings more despicable, yet you would scarcely believe how the Germans are pleased with them. They sing, shout, dance, and jump, so that the stove seems ready to fall. No one can hear another speak. But it seems to please them, and you are obliged to sit there, whether you will or not, until midnight.

A. Now you must finish the entertainment; for I am also worn out with the length of it.

B. Very well. When at last the cheese, which hardly pleases them unless rotten and full of worms, has been taken away, the bearded fellow appears, bearing a trencher on which are drawn with chalk some circles and semi-circles, and he lays it upon the table, so silent, meanwhile, and sad, that you would say he was some Charon. Then they who comprehend the meaning of this lay down their money, one after another, until the trencher is filled. Then having observed who has contributed, he counts it silently; and if nothing is wanting he nods his head.

B. What if there should be too much?

A. Perhaps he would return it. As a matter of fact, this is sometimes done.

B. Does nobody ever complain about the counting as unjust?

A. Nobody who is prudent. For he would hear at once: "What sort of a fellow are you? You are paying no more than the others!"

B. This is certainly a frank kind of people you are telling about.

A. And if anybody, weary with his journey, asks to go to bed soon after supper, he is ordered to wait until the rest also go to bed.

B. I seem to see a Platonic city.

A. Then each is shown to his rest, and it is truly nothing more than a bed room; for there is nothing there but a bed, and nothing else that you can use or steal.

B. Is there cleanliness?

A. Just as at dinner; linen washed six months ago, perhaps.

B. In the meantime what had become of the horses?

A. They were treated according to the same method as the men.

B. But do you get the same accommodations everywhere?

A. Sometimes more courteous, sometimes harsher than I have told you; but on the whole it is as I have said.

B. How would you like me to tell you how guests are treated in that part of Italy which is called Lombardy, or in Spain, or in England and in Wales? For the English have assimilated in part the French and in part the German customs, being a mixture of these two nations. The Welsh boast that they are the original English.

A. I should like you to tell me, for I have never had occasion to see them.

B. At present I have not time, for the sailor told me to meet him at three o'clock, or I should be left behind; and he has my baggage. Some other time we shall have an opportunity of chatting to our hearts' content.

CHAPTER XV

Conversion

After many years of playing the part of a genuine humanist, Erasmus saw the grave error of his ways and suddenly made a serious turn in the direction he had been facing ever since he had arrived at the College of Montaigu in Paris. One result of his dramatic conversion was the composition of his last colloquy entitled, *The Epicurean*. Its title has for centuries intrigued many intelligent critics who realized that the man whom Erasmus had taken as his guide in the realm of thinking and living was not all Epicurean by any means. Already in his first book on the contempt of the world he had quoted Epicurus as a model in the art of decent living. It seems that there was some difference in the minds of Erasmus and his contemporaries between the life and beliefs of Epicurus himself and those persons who were actually called Epicurean.

Unfortunately the experts in the field of the Northern Renaissance have very seldom discussed the remarkable change in the attitude adopted by Erasmus near the end of his life. These experts should have observed the terrific contrast between his views as expressed in Chapter XII of *De Contemptu Mundi* as well as the second version of *The Book Against The Barbarians*, and those advanced in his *Catechism*. In the latter he simply contradicted the humanistic philosophy exhibited by him in 1497 and 1521. We are not a bit surprised to note his attitude expressed in the colloquy entitled, *The Epicurean* (1533). One speaker is called Hedonius, for he supports hedonism, which means the pursuit of pleasure. The other's name is Spudaeus, since he recommends common sense. Hedonius says this: "No school attracts me more than the Epicurean . . . Epicurus was whatever you please, and consider the matter in itself. Human happiness, so he holds, is the product of pleasure, and he deems that life most blessed which has the most pleasure and the least sorrow." We are following here the version by Thompson on p. 538. Then Spudaeus admits that this is the case.

At this point Hedonius comes up with an astonishing idea: "What judgment could have been more holy than this?" Even more intriguing is the following remark by Hedonius: "There are no people more Epicurean than godly Christians." In this connection we must quote a few lines from the famous book by Will Durant, *The Story of Philosophy*. On p. 112 he says this: "Epicurus, then, is no epicurean; he exalts the joys of intellect rather than those of sense; he warns against pleasures that excite and disturb the soul which they should rather quiet and appease. In the end he proposes to seek not pleasure in its usual sense, but *ataraxia* – tranquility, equanimity, repose of mind; all of which trembles on the verge of Zeno's 'apathy.'" That is exactly what Erasmus had said about him in his first book: *De Contemptu Mundi*. But we have just quoted his strange remark to the effect that "there are no people more Epicurean than godly Christians."

Equally confusing is the next statement by Hedonius: "Those who have washed away their stains by the lye of tears and the soap of repentance or the fire of charity are not only unharmed by sins but they often pave the way to greater good." Spudaeus now says this: "Do those whom Christ calls 'blessed' because they mourn live a life of pleasure?" And Hedonius answers as follows: "To the world they appear to mourn, but in fact they're joyful and live agreeably." He also claims that "true pleasure befalls only a sane person." Completely opposed to the Epicurean philosophy is another remark by Hedonius: "How much stronger must be that heavenly love proceeding from the spirit of Christ. So great is its power that even death – than which nothing is more dreadful – is made pleasing."

Hedonius grows more and more anti-Epicurean and more and more in favor of dynamic Christianity as he goes on like this: "No one lives enjoyably unless he lives righteously; that is, enjoys true goods." Equally pro-Christian is the next proposition: "Now just see how very far from pleasure are those who openly pursue nothing but pleasures. In the first place, their minds are stained and corrupted by the leaven of lusts, so that if anything sweet does happen to them it turns sour at once, as water from a polluted well necessarily has a bad taste. Secondly, there's no true pleasure except what is comprehended by a sound mind." On p. 546 we find still more anti-Epicureanism as expressed by Hedonius: "Since they understand that everything is sent by God either to cleanse us of faults or to test our virtue, they receive it not only patiently but gladly, as obedient sons from the hand of a gracious father; and they even give thanks, whether for his merciful chastisement or for their inestimable gain." Finally, here comes genuine Stoicism: "Since their minds are disciplined to temperance and endurance, they bear unavoidable ills more steadfastly than others do."

Erasmus did not always write like this before the year 1532. We note, for example, accusations made by the famous Lefèvre before February 22, 1518, when Erasmus wrote to Budé about them: "But after, – not to speak of other harsh words, – he had made me 'contumelious against Christ,' 'a subverter of the Prophetic intelligence,' 'a partisan of Judaism,' 'unworthily debasing the dignity of Christ,' 'opposing the spirit, and adhering to the flesh and to the letter, 'saying things inconsistent and subversive of one another, and that against the glory of Christ,' ... I submit them to your judgment."[1] Here we suspect that Lefèvre, like many other celebrated characters, took the liberty to exaggerate the wicked language of our hero. During the past 50 years the present writer has often expressed disapproval of certain actions and written statements by Erasmus which were not to the latter's credit. But now the time has come to look at the "other side of the picture."

We shall in this connection discuss once more the notorious dialogue entitled, *Julius Excluded*. Once more we shall publish the statement which first appeared in the essay published in front of the second edition of the book on young Erasmus: "Why should Erasmus have suggested that the pope acquire 'gorgeous whores, the most accommodating pimps?' How could Erasmus have stated that 'so few come to this place [Rome], when pestilences like this sit at the helm of the Church?'" Moreover, the salacious author wrote that the people "honor this filthy sewer because he bears the title of Pope." Nowhere in Erasmus' writings now known to us can we find such ghastly accusations against any pope in person.[2]

Very seldom has any competent writer presented a suitable analysis of the report on the scandalous dialogue addressed by Erasmus himself to Cardinal Wolsey, the exact date being May 18, 1517. He wrote as follows: "Several months ago an ill-starred and ridiculous booklet came out, the subject of which sufficiently shows that it was written upon the last vacancy of the Papal See, but by what writer is not known, save that

---

[1] D. Erasmus, *Epistles*, ed. F. M. Nichols, Vol. III, pp. 264-264.
[2] A. Hyma, *The Youth of Erasmus* (1968 ed.), p. XIII. See also the essay by Roland H. Bainton in the Festschrift in honor of Franz Lau (Berlin, 1967), p. 17-25: "Erasmus and Luther and the Dialog Julius Exclusus." Here Bainton says on p. 17 that Erasmus was the author of the poem we have mentioned above, but he has taken proper note of Stange's book.

its contents show, that, whoever it was, his sympathies were with the French." That is exactly what the present writer stated in the second edition of his book on young Erasmus even before he had ever read the letter which we are now discussing.[1] Erasmus continued by saying that "the suspicion of its authorship goes the round of many different persons, especially among the Germans, the work being current among them under various titles. When I met with it here myself some years ago circulated in a furtive way, and had some taste of its contents, – for I galloped through it rather than read it, – many persons can bear witness how hateful it was to me, and what pains I took, that it should be hidden in eternal darkness, – a thing that has been done by me more than once, in the case of other publications, as many persons will admit."

At this point Erasmus says that he has referred to this work before in his letter to John Caesarius, "which was published at Cologne from a copy furtively obtained." So now we must peruse this letter in order to determine just what Erasmus had written at that time. We find it in Vol. II of the correspondence of Erasmus issued by Francis Morgan Nichols.[2] Here we read this: "I highly disapproved of the *Epistles of Obscure Men*. Their pleasantry might amuse at first glance, if such a precedent had not been too aggressive. I have no objection to the ludicrous, provided it be without insult to any one." That remark is well worth serious study on the part of those writers who in recent years have insinuated that Erasmus in *The Praise of Folly* actually and specifically referred to Pope Julius II.[3]

As for our dialogue, Erasmus remarks that in the second edition of *The Letters of Obscure Men* his name "was mixed up in it: as if it were not enough to play the fool, without exposing us to prejudice, and in a great measure destroying the fruit obtained by so much laborious study." That being the case, we can well understand his anger when he has to make this remark about the dialog in question: "There is some sort of publication in the hands of many persons in Cologne, directed against Pope Julius, and representing him as excluded by St. Peter from heaven ... I wonder what people are thinking of, when they waste their leisure and their labour in such a way. But I am still more surprised that there are persons who suspect, that such signal folly has proceeded from me. I attribute this to the fact, that the language used is perhaps not such bad Latin."

---

[1] A. Hyma, *The Youth of Erasmus* (1968), p. XI.
[2] D. Erasmus, *Letters*, ed. Nichols, Vol. II (1962), pp. 610-612.
[3] One of them was Professor Jesse K. Sowards. See above in Chapter I.

It seems strange that Mr. Nichols, in editing this material, draws a hazardous conclusion of his own. He states that the *Julius Exclusus* "was undoubtedly the work of Erasmus." He bases his opinion on the fact that Erasmus had actually made a copy of it, which copy he had left with Lupset and More. The latter reported to him as follows: "Lupset has restored to me some sheets of yours, which he had kept by him for some time. Among them is the *Genius of Julius* . . . All are in your hand."[1] This fact was well known to the present writer when he discussed the authorship of the dialogue in the essay on the subject in the front of his book on young Erasmus.[2]

The latter was consistent in his *Praise of Folly* wherever he discussed the papacy, or the evils of his own time. He said himself that such was indeed the case, as the present writer indicated in the essay of his just mentioned. Why should he "stick out his neck," so to speak? He was too clever a diplomat to antagonize any pope in particular, and especially his two benefactors, Julius II and Leo X. The same is true of his attitude toward archbishops, kings, dukes, counts, and rectors of the leading universities. It is astonishing to read in his correspondence of his friendship with King Henry VIII, the archbishop of Canterbury, the outstanding scholars in several countries, and many sorts of great ambassadors, legates, and legislators. Moreover, the immense circulation of his books indicates a greater influence than any other European writer in medieval and modern times. Furthermore, we are happy at this stage to report his sensational conversion from a life of weak moral principles to a much higher level, as indicated in the colloquy entitled, "The Epicurean" and his book known as the *Catechism*, both produced in the year 1533.

Professor William James Hirten of Siena College at Loudonville, N.Y. in the year 1967 published a reprint of Erasmus' first book, *On the Contempt of the World*, the English translation of 1533, as we saw above. He stated that "in order to arrange with Jerome Froben for the publication of the *Ecclesiastes*, Erasmus came to Basel in 1535. He met his end giving definite evidence of true piety and a spirit of Christian resignation." Hirten goes on to say that he now was strongly in favor of monasticism: "Highly praising the members of these orders (Carthusians and Brigittines) for the austerity of their lives, which is never abated 'even when they are dwelling in the coldest regions,' he asks: 'When

---

[1] D. Erasmus, *Letters*, Nichols ed., Vol. II, pp. 446-447.
[2] A. Hyma, *The Youth of Erasmus*, pp. VI-VII.

so many men like these willingly take upon themselves such austerities in order to deserve well of Christ, why are there so few who strive eagerly for the office of preacher?' "[1]

Now the question arises as to what Erasmus had in mind when he composed the first version of *De Contemptu Mundi* in or about the year 1490. He was sincere in praising monasticism at that time. But why did he keep on quoting Epicurus rather than St. Augustine or St. Jerome? His closest friends must have urged him to study the Church Fathers rather than a man like Epicurus. At any rate, he continued in the year 1533 to praise Epicurus and the Epicureans while defending the orthodox Christian religion. We have quoted some sections from the strange colloquy entitled, "The Epicurian." Now we shall add some more comments drawn from the edition by C. R. Thompson: "Epicurus accepted the atomic theory of Democritus and revised the ethical doctrine of Aristippus. He taught that pleasure is the only good. Pleasure is to be sought deliberately. But not all pleasures are equally desirable. The most desirable are intellectual, not sensual, and are best cultivated in a life of simplicity and retirement." Thompson himself is puzzled by Erasmus' seemingly strange use of the term "Epicurean." For Erasmus must have known that his confusing explanation was contrary to accepted customs among his own colleagues at Steyn. Says Thompson: "Of course the paradox succeeds solely on condition that we limit ourselves to the ethical side of Epicureanism, ignoring its physics, and accept the rhetorical cast of the argument rather than scrutinize its logic too closely.[2]

What Thompson in the year 1965, when he published his admirable edition of the *Colloquies*, did not realize was that Erasmus during the academic year 1532-1533 was converted to a new type of religion for himself. Thus far, even from 1486 to 1492, he had never been an orthodox Christian. Particularly when in 1517 he argued that it would have been a good thing if his brother Peter had hanged himself, he gave vent to feelings of inner rebellion against "the establishment." Just why did his parents have to give him such a terrible start in his youth, especially in the little town of Gouda? We are not a bit surprised to learn that it was perfectly natural for him in the year 1497 to express great contempt for the leading professors at the Sorbonne. Nor were

---

[1] Erasmus, *On the Contempt of the World*, ed. of 1533 (1967), pp. xxxix-xl.
[2] D. Erasmus, *Colloquies*, ed. C. R. Thompson, pp. 535-537.

we astonished when we studied his neurotic attachments at Montaigu and the English boarding-house in its vicinity.

Thompson throws welcome light upon our intriguing problem with the following report: "For a century before Erasmus wrote his colloquy there had been intermittent debate among humanists about the merits of the Epicurean doctrine of pleasure. This debate began with Lorenzo Valla's dialogue, *De voluptate* (1441), which presents arguments for Stoic, Epicurean, and Christian ethics. The spokesman for Christian ethics is allowed to win, but to some readers Valla's eloquence on behalf of Epicurean naturalism and his assumed preference for this over Christian asceticism are more impressive than his conventional or prudent award of victory to Christianity." Thompson argues correctly that the defender of Epicureanism "denounces celibacy and approves of sexual liberty."

Hedonius, according to Thompson, "purports to demonstrate that Christian and classical values are not mutually exclusive or totally irreconcilable." The classical values "must be tested and refined by Christian knowledge before their full potentialities can be realized." This sounds most reasonable and convincing when we observe that Erasmus in the year 1533 was in the process of a genuine conversion. He was no longer interested in harmonizing orthodox Christianity with classical Greek and Roman civilization. The latter had been worshiped long enough by him. Now let us examine an illuminating statement in the famous book by Bataillon, *Erasme et l'Espagne*, as quoted on p. 128 in the article by Thomas N. Tentler, "Erasmus on Forgiveness and Consolation," in *Studies in the Renaissance*, Vol. XII (1965): "The time for laughing had passed. If his thought had not varied since the *Colloquies*, the irony of 'The Funeral' was no longer appropriate. The being Erasmus prepared for death was every man, and particularly himself."

Consequently, our next objective must be to examine the Colloquy named "The Funeral," first published in 1526. Here Erasmus is not yet on the verge of conversion. He can still concentrate upon entertainment, and so he presents a striking contrast between the death of a serious-minded Christian and a "man of the world." Particularly amusing is the quarrel among the physicians, who first acted like vultures in exacting their large fees and then quarreled among themselves as to the nature of the dying man's illness. Moreover, there was also an amusing contest between the priest who heard the last confession and the parish priest. The former was a Franciscan Friar, and obviously the parish priest insisted upon hearing the confession before he was willing to present the Extreme Unction. That, as we said, was written in the year 1526.

Very different is the account in Erasmus' last colloquy. Here we note that the name of one speaker is Spudaeus, meaning, as Thompson tells us, Serious. The other speaker, as we saw, was Hedonius. Spudaeus says that the Epicurean School "is more universally detested than any other." Consequently, he is puzzled when Hedonius says that no school attracts him more than the Epicurean. No wonder he is puzzled, for such talk had seldom been advanced. Consequently, Hedonius must be on his guard, and he wisely contends that they must not quibble about bad reputations. He is very clever in arguing that "Epicurus was whatever you please – and consider the matter in itself." Here then comes a sensible remark by Hedonius: "When young men get from whoring the new disease now euphemistically called the 'Neapolitan itch' – and generally they do get it – through which they are so often doomed to a living death, always carrying a living corpse about, don't they seem to *Epicurize* beautifully? Spudaeus. Not at all; they seem to be looking for a cure. Hedonius. Now weigh the pleasure against the pain: would you want the agony of a toothache for as long as the pleasure of drinking or whoring lasted? Spudaeus. Well, I'd prefer to do without both, for to buy pleasure with pain is not getting but spending."

Next Hedonius comes up with a pertinent comment: "Poverty, a heavy and miserable burden, is the constant companion of gluttony; paralysis, palsy, inflammation of the eyes, blindness, and leprosy – and not only these – of intemporate sexual indulgence." Then Spudaeus says that "even if no torture resulted, one who exchanged jewels for glass would seem to be a very foolish bargainer." His friend now asks if he means that such a person would "sacrifice the true goods of the mind to the deceitful pleasures of the body." So Spudaeus answers that this is his opinion. And Hedonius then adds another idea: "Torment of conscience and we've agreed there's nothing worse – *is* always the companion of unlawful pleasure." Erasmus also takes proper care of the arguments he now wants to use in favor of monasticism: "This Franciscan, barefoot, girded with a knotted cord, poorly and cheaply dressed, worn by fasting, vigils, and labors, without a penny in the world, lives more delightfully – provided only that he has a good conscience – than six hundred Sardanapaluses rolled into one."

In the foregoing conversations we witness indeed a change of heart on the part of the writer. And also the last paragraph continues to reveal what Erasmus in the year 1533 believed about orthodox Christianity.

No longer does he insinuate that those who were virtuous before they entered a monastery became immoral after their entrance there, nor that those who had been willing to live for many years with a cantankerous wife would become hopelessly addicted to lust after joining the monks somewhere. On the contrary, we read this at the end: "With how few words the dying thief won paradise from Christ! If he cries with his whole heart, 'Have mercy on me, O God, according to the multitude of thy tender mercies,' the Lord will take away the Tantalean stone, will grant him the sound of joy and gladness, and his bones broken by contrition shall rejoice for sins forgiven."[1]

Erasmus saw too late that he had squandered valuable resources while he was traveling in his humanistic paradise, especially of course when he was a student at the Sorbonne. There he scorned the advice given to him by Professor Gryllard, as he said himself during the year 1497 in his letter addressed to Thomas Grey. He also indulged in a terrible hatred of a disagreeable person in the English boarding-house to which he had moved when leaving the College of Montaigu. It seems that this quarrel forced him to look for other quarters, about which we now know very little. At any rate, we must examine a few phrases in a letter he wrote to Father Nicholas Werner at Steyn near Gouda: "If you are all well at Steyn, it is what we wish and trust . . . I have lately fallen in with some Englishmen, all of noble birth and high rank. Very lately a young man in priest's orders joined the party. He had abundance of money, and had refused a bishopric, because he was aware of his deficiency in learning . . . When he heard of my knowledge of Letters, he began to exhibit an incredible regard and respect for me; for he lived some little time in my household . . . He offered me a benefice within a few months. . . . If I had chosen to accept his proposals, I should have obliged all the English in this city, for they are all of the highest families, and through them all England."[2]

But he turned down all offers at that time, which must have been in the month of September 1496, for the letter is dated September 13, 1496. He claimed that his overwhelming desire was to obtain "a doctorate in theology." On November 7, 1496, he wrote an important letter to Henry of Bergen, the bishop of Cambrai, about whom we have said a great deal in connection with the composition of the *Book Against the Barbarians*. He reported that he had been away from Paris in order

---

[1] D. Erasmus, *Colloquies*, ed. C. R. Thompson, pp. 538-551.
[2] D. Erasmus, *Letters*, ed. Nichols, Vol. I, pp. 117-118.

to publish a collection of poems by William of Gouda. He also mentioned the sad fact that he had been very ill while still living in the English boardinghouse. Moreover, Father Werner had informed him that some of his colleagues at Steyn disapproved of his studies. We should note here that in the year 1514, when he was ordered to return to Steyn, he reported that he was too ill to go back to the severe climate in the County of Holland. This sad subject we have discussed above.

In February 1497 he told William of Gouda that he had "lately fallen ill after a journey." He proudly added that he was living with "a most courteous English gentleman, together with two young men of good condition." Very significant is the following sentence: "It is now three months since I have paid a visit to Faustus or Gaguin." We have stated above that Faustus Andrelini was the author of *Julius Exclusus*, while Gaguin composed the famous work on the history of France. The pro-French attitude of Faustus we have explained above. Erasmus, as we saw, also was very well aware of that subject. On the other hand, the Bishop of Utrecht, so Erasmus claimed in February 1497, was "a niggardly man." That will explain an important reason why the Dutch humanist had to depend upon financial support rendered by several English patrons, rather than Dutch noblemen. And Henry of Bergen was a native of Brabant, not Holland, or Utrecht! Brabant then included the cities of Brussels and Louvain.

In this connection we shall analyze the following report made by Robert P. Adams in his book, *The Better Part of Valor*, which book we have mentioned several times above: "Hyma would have us believe, on the one hand, that the English humanists had slight influence upon the Netherlander and, on the other, demolish the idea that Erasmus had a great deal to do with the development of English humanism."[1] Hyma after 1969 became convinced that Erasmus exerted more influence in England than he had previously understood. Now let us see what else Erasmus added in support of the writer's theory. Mr. Nichols informs us that "Lord Mountjoy was recalled home about April, 1497, for the celebration of his wedding, his mother and guardian, the countess of Ormond, having arranged a marriage for him with Elizabeth, one of the daughters and presumptive heirs of Sir William Say, a rich proprietor in Hertfordshire."

Nichols also serves us very well in reporting that Erasmus had a

---

[1] R. P. Adams, *op. cit.*, 25.

serious quarrel with the head of the English boarding-house where he had met several prominent young Englishmen. Nichols is correct in asserting that "the extreme violence of his language may lead to the suspicion that he was in the wrong." Let us then examine some of that astonishing language: "When offended at the barbarous sound, you exclaimed, What devil's name is that?... His history is this. Having diligently spent his whole life in the practice of every sort of wickedness, so as to fear no competition with any thief or impostor, he reached that profciency in his trade, as to fill the part of traitor at Paris on behalf of his king. This is a class for which no one is fit who is not a thorough traitor ... And, not to detain you longer, this half-Scot is the assassin of our Erasmus."[1]

Nichols says that the greater part of Erasmus' letter to Thomas Grey, dated August 1497, "is therefore omitted in the following translation." We might have consulted the original version as published by P. S. Allen, but we shall merely quote some of the lesser poison: "Considering my friendship, my services, my loyalty, my almost fraternal love, when could I ever have expected such a signal indignity from a man grey, noble, as he boasts himself, and religious, as he pretends to be?... If you can ever love a monster of the kind, you will be the most fickle of mortals; if you really mean it, you will be the greatest of fools, if you do it for adulation, the meanest of flatterers."[2] In another letter he advises Grey to study Virgil, Lucan, Cicero, Lactantius, Jerome, Sallust, and Livy.[3] He ridicules scholasticism in the following terms: "I, who have always been a primitive Theologian, have begun of late to be a Scotist... Hush, profane one, thou knowest nothing of theological slumber. There are many that in their sleep not only write, but slander and get drunk, and commit other indiscretions... Most divines of our time never wake at all; and when they sleep on mandragora, they think themselves most awake."[4] We have observed above that the young humanist accused the top professors at the Sorbonne of having rotten brains. Here are a few more choice morsels: "If you have touched good letters, you must unlearn what you have learned... I do my best to speak nothing in true Latin, nothing elegant or witty."

Equally disappointing is our study of two letters addressed to the Lady of Veere, who was one of his patrons around the year 1500, and to

[1] D. Erasmus, *Letters*, ed. Nichols, Vol. I, pp. 131-134.
[2] D. Erasmus, *Letters*, ed. Nichols, Vol. I, p. 139.
[3] *Ibidem*, p. 140.
[4] *Ibidim*, p. 142.

James Batt, who knew her very well. In the first one he wrote as follows: "Three Annas have been commended to posterity by ancient literature... May heaven grant such virtue to my writings, that posterity, not unacquainted with your pious, chaste, and stainless heart, may number a fourth Anna with the other three."[1] Contrasted with this brazen flattery we note a very different description of her character in the letter addressed to Batt. There our hero said this: "She has the means to keep those cowled libertines and good for nothing scoundrels, – you know whom I mean, – and not means to maintain the leisure of one who can write books which even posterity may value, if I speak somewhat boastfully of myself. She has fallen, I fear, into some straits. It is her own fault, as she has chosen to associate with that insignificant coxcomb, rather than with a grave and serious companion suitable to her sex and age."[2]

Very different was the aged Erasmus when he dedicated his *Catechism* to the father of Anne Boleyn in England. This, as we saw, happened in the year 1533. Moreover, during the next year he came up with one of his most popular works, namely, *Preparation for Death*. We shall once more refer to the illuminating article entitled, "Erasmus on Forgiveness and Consolation," published by Professor Thomas N. Tentler in Volume XII of *Studies in the Renaissance* (1965). The latter informs us that "at least thirty-two editions appeared within ten years after its publication." Erasmus "returns here to the *Imitation*. He tells the dying man to emulate Christ, who submitted to His Father's will at the time of the passion. All human affections must be ignored. The keys to eternal peace are faith, hope, and charity." Tentler also refers to "the philosophy of Christ."[3]

During the last four years of his life Erasmus sought to make up for his attachment to humanism. The present writer in his advanced classes dealing with the Renaissance and the Reformation on the campus at the University of Michigan (and especially in his extension courses at Detroit, Grand Rapids, Flint, Pontiac, Saginaw, Bay City, Port Huron, and Mount Clemens) always emphasized the enormous change in the character of Erasmus between 1525 and 1536.

---

[1] *Ibidem*, p. 294.
[2] D. Erasmus, *Letters*, ed. Nichols, Vol. I, p. 306.
[3] Thomas N. Tentler, *op. cit.*, pp. 131-132.

CHAPTER XVI

On the Separation of Church and State

It must seem puzzling to note that today our two most famous Protestant theologians in the United States of America still give the Reformation rather than the Northern Renaissance the credit for having produced the separation of Church and State. The Rev. Norman Vincent Peale stated in the leading article of *Reader's Digest* dated September 1962 that among the greatest blessings our nation has received from the Reformation was the separation of Church and State. In doing so he misled millions of devout persons. The same sort of thing was finally accomplished by Billy Graham when on April 25, 1966, he repeated what his chief competitor among American Protestants had already stated. On the front page of *United States News & World Report* a large picture of the famous evangelist appeared, calling attention to his admirable article entitled, "God is Not Dead." The two Protestant dictators proudly proclaimed the false doctrine just mentioned, much the the chagrin of their Roman Catholic rivals. Their grateful followers never seriously considered the obvious fact that neither of them had ever taken the pains to study the original sources in Europe which plainly indicated that it was Erasmus and his supporters who fashioned the new idea. Unfortunately no amount of religious fervor can replace original records of historical events like the Belgic Confession and the Treaty of Augsburg signed in 1555.

In the year 1860 John Lothrop Motley declared on p. 35 of Vol. 1 in his great work entitled, *History of the United Netherlands*, the exact truth about the Lutherans in Germany: "The princes had got the Augsburg Confession and the abbey-lands into the bargain; the peasants had got the Augsburg Confession without the abbey-lands, and were to believe what their masters believed. This was the German-Lutheran sixteenth-century idea of religious freedom." Motley was referring to the notorious Latin phrase in the Treaty of Augsburg (1555), which ended the religious wars in the Holy Roman Empire: "*Cuius regio, eius religio.*" This meant that he who was the ruler in a certain region was permitted to force all of his subjects to join his particular denomination. Moreover, the Belgic Confession, which is the official creed of the *Hervormde Kerk* and the *Gereformeerde Kerk* in the Netherlands, plus the Reformed Church of America and the Christian Reformed Church, states that civil rulers have the right to compel their subjects to join their respective churches. This was stated in the notorious Article 36. The Rev. Leonard Verduin has stated on p. 122 of *The Twentieth Century Encyclopedia of Religious Knowledge* that "the Reformed Church of America has simply recast the article in what was intended to be a translation, so getting rid of the problem," while the Christian Reformed Church "turned the trick by adding a footnote in which the matters confessed in the text were forthwith repudiated." Later on he was charged with the task of revising this article for his own denomination. Under the direction of the present writer he also issued an article on Guido de Brès, who was the author of the Belgic Confession, and the present writer composed the article on the Treaty of Augsburg.

The Reformation was directly responsible for the official creeds of the Reformed and Lutheran churches, while the Church of England in its present form is also a product of the Reformation. It is well known that the Queen of Great Britain would lose her official position as queen if she should leave the Church of England. It should also be noted here that in the colony of New Netherland the only church that was officially recognized was the Dutch Reformed Church. The present writer in his book entitled, *Christianity and Politics*, has this illuminating passage: "Whenever a group of persons attempted to form another, the Reformed churches took swift action in Amsterdam, harassing the directors of the West India Company until the latter prohibited the founding of another denomination." Moreover, the established church in New England (Congregational) remained the state supported church until well into the nineteenth century. "It was not until 1833 that in Massachusetts state support was withdrawn from the Congregational Church." Moreover, the present writer in his book just mentioned states that "one important obstacle in the path toward full democracy in New England had been the stipulation that only church members were permitted to vote on important questions."[1]

Consequently, the time has now come to face the actual facts in the development of real religious liberty as envisioned by Erasmus and his

---

[1] A. Hyma, *op. cit.*, pp. 310-315.

followers. One of the most important contributions of the Northern Renaissance has been the separation of Church and State. Thus far this contribution has very seldom been carefully studied by either historians or theologians. Neither Roman Catholic nor Protestant leaders have had the slightest understanding of this extremely important feature of the Northern Renaissance. One chief cause of misunderstanding has been the lack of interest in the Northern Renaissance, and especially Erasmus himself.

Preserved Smith on pp. 199-201 of his splendid biography of Erasmus quoted some pertinent remarks by Erasmus in his *Adages* issued in 1515: "The eagle is the image of the king, for he is neither beautiful nor musical nor fit for food, but he is carnivorous, rapacious, a brigand, a destroyer, solitary, hated by all, a pest to all, who, though he can do more harm than anyone, wishes to do more than he can . . . In both ancient and modern history, and in any period comprising but a few centuries, hardly one or two princes are to be found whose signal folly did not inflict ruin on mankind . . . We trust the rudder of a vessel in which but a few sailors and some goods are in danger, to none but skillful pilots; but the state, wherein the safety of so many thousands is at stake, is put into any hands that chance has provided." Here Erasmus is obviously referring to the inheritance of a throne by an incompetent heir. He also said this: "A charioteer must learn, study, and practise his art; but a prince needs merely to be born." It was partly because of the enormous influence of Erasmus in his native land that the Dutch people transferred the sovereignty of their new nation from the King of Spain to the President of the Dutch Republic. In all directions there were to be found kings and dukes and counts. But the Dutch alone set forth upon the path of republicanism, turning the counties of Holland, Zeeland, and Friesland into provinces, while the Duchy of Gelderland also became a province. This fascinating transformation has seldom been studied properly by either historians or political scientists.

Once more we shall quote Erasmus himself, and now from the world-famous *Praise of Folly*: "He that sits at the helm of the government acts in a public capacity, and so must sacrifice all private interest to the attainment of the common good. He must himself be conformable to those laws his prerogative exacts, or else he can expect no obedience to be paid to them by others. He must have a strict eye over all his inferior magistrates and officers, or otherwise it is not to be doubted that they will carelessly discharge their respective duties."[1]

[1] A. Hyma, *Christianity and Politics*, p. 90.

Erasmus makes fun of those people who adore their beloved but selfish and incompetent kings: "Hang about his neck a gold chain, for an intimation that he ought to have all virtues linked together; then set a crown of gold and jewels on his head, for a token that he ought to overtop and outshine others in the commendable qualifications; next, put into his hand a royal scepter for a symbol of justice and integrity; lastly, clothe him with purple, for a hieroglyphic of a tender love and affection for the commonwealth." Erasmus also was extremely effective in pointing out all the defects in monarchical governments. He complained energetically about the hunting and sports engaged in by kings and dukes and counts: "They think they have sufficiently acquitted themselves in the duty of governing if they but go constantly hunting, breed good race-horses, sell places and offices to those courtiers who will give most for them, and find new ways for invading their people's property, and securing a larger revenue for their own exchequer."[1]

Motley on p. 5 of his great work just mentioned writes as follows: "There was a country which believed in the absolute power of the church to dictate the relations between man and his Maker, and to utterly exterminate all who disputed that position. There was another country which protested against that doctrine, and claimed, theoretically or practically, a liberty of conscience. The territory of these countries was mapped out by no visible lines, but the inhabitants of each, whether resident in France, Germany, England, or Flanders, recognized a relationship which took its root in deeper differences than those of race or language. A large portion of the world had become tired of the antiquated delusion of papal supremacy over every land, and had recorded its determination, once and for all, to have done with it. The transition to freedom of conscience became a necessary step, sooner or later to be taken. To establish the principle of toleration for all religions was an inevitable consequence of the Dutch revolt."

Next we must quote from another famous book produced in the United States of America: *Erasmus A Study of His Life, Ideals and Place in History*, by Preserved Smith. On p. 209 he writes as follows: "Erasmus laid the eggs and Luther hatched the chickens." Next we have this: "Erasmus is the father of Luther." And again we quote some more: "Aleander asserted that Luther and Erasmus taught the same things, save that the poison of the latter was more deadly." And on the Protestant side we get similar exaggerations. Smith now quotes from Conrad Mutianus:

[1] *Ibidem*, p. 91.

"We all know that we must congratulate theology on being restored by Erasmus, from whom, as from a fountain, are derived Oecolampadii, Melancthons, Luthers, and oh! how many princes in literature!" Nevertheless, Preserved Smith on the next page states correctly that "the Reformation was the child of more than one ancestor." Thus it becomes our task and duty to distinguish among many different sources just which really produced the separation of Church and State. We must recognize here now the work done by the Northern Renaissance under the leadership of Erasmus.

Preserved Smith on p. 244 expresses his personal opinion about the attitude taken by Erasmus toward the Reformation, which differs somewhat from that of the present writer: "In the opinion of the present writer, Erasmus' attitude toward the Reformation was wrong, because the present writer thinks that the Reformation was justified in its purpose and on the whole good in its results. With all his faults and all his sins, Luther acted a nobler, more heroic, and also a historically more justifiable part than did Erasmus. Not only was he braver, but he was ultimately more right in his judgment of the requirements of the time and of the remedies suitable for restoring health and vitality to suffering Christendom." It so happened that both sides fell far short of the high ideals produced by that wonderful intellectual movement which we have called the Northern Renaissance. Even Erasmus himself did not do justice to the great masters in the Devotio Moderna. He was never able to extricate from his character the tendencies displayed by him when he was a student at the Sorbonne. When the latter institution condemned some of his colloquies up to the year 1533, he gradually gave up his antagonism toward the leaders at the University of Paris. Thus followed his conversion, as we saw in the preceding chapter. Unfortunately this episode has seldom been properly elucidated by either Roman Catholic or Protestant theologians and historians.

We have just seen that Erasmus strongly supported the principle which now widely prevails in the United States of America. It is well understood among both theologians and historians that neither a civil servant of our people nor an ecclesiastical potentate should be permitted to acquire the title to his office solely through the process of heredity. But the great Protestant leaders of the sixteenth and seventeenth ceturies failed to acquire our high ideals in this respect. They continued, as we saw, to favor a close relationship between Church and State. Even as late as in the year 1555 it was agreed in the Treaty of Augsburg by the outstanding Protestants that the old system must be continued. Let us quote here a few sentences from the article on the Treaty of Augsburg in *The Twentieth Century Encyclopedia of Religious Knowledge* by the present writer: "Here the strange concept of *Cuius regio eius religio* was expressed for the first time in a definitive and legal way. During the past three decades a number of experts in political science, especially in the United States, have concluded that Martin Luther was largely responsible for the idea that the prince may dictate to his subjects what their religious views must be and what sort of books they shall read in the field of religion. The Treaty of Augsburg in 1555 was, however, the outcome of local political conditions and the revival of the study of Roman Law (*Corpus Juris Civilis* by Emperor Justinian). Luther in 1523 published a treatise on the subject that contained exactly the opposite of *cuius regio eius religio* (*On Civil Government: In How Far One Should Obey It*). He as well as his most intimate followers, together with their opponents also, were carried along in the tide toward absolutism, very slowly as first, and after Luther's death much more rapidly." This was a far cry from the sentiments espressed by Erasmus in several of his publications.

Next we shall quote from another article among the 185 which the present writer issued in the encyclopedia just mentioned. This one deals with the career of Erasmus: "When Luther and Melanchthon began to rely upon the support of their elector to suppress heresy in Saxony, Erasmus frowned upon such measures. He wanted above all things tolerance and individual freedom. Luther shuddered when he first read the 'big seller' of the time, *Praise of Folly*, in which Erasmus ridiculed sacred practices and beliefs. On many occasions Erasmus felt amused, while Luther was profoundly grieved."

Much more important, however, is the present writer's section on the Northern Renaissance on p. 964. Here we read this: "Those who are interested in the growth of capitalistic society, of modern democracy, and of religious and political liberty will find in the Northern Renaissance a wealth of source material for serious and fruitful study. Over against the autocracy and intolerance of the sixteenth century they can place the valiant fight for popular sovereignty and personal liberty waged by Gansfort, Erasmus and Cusa (*q.v.*). In both church and state these men recommended local autonomy and individual rights. Gansfort and Erasmus argued that kings were bound by their contracts with the subjects they ruled, and Erasmus argued that princes should not be permitted to inherit their power to rule."

Another section deals with a comparison between the enlightened views of Erasmus and Gansfort as compared with those of other humanists and reformers: "The fact is that Luther and Calvin reflected the shortcomings of their age, whereas men like Gansfort, More, and Erasmus looked beyond the sixteenth century to the nineteenth for true liberty and democracy. The three men just mentioned believed in human depravity but not in total depravity. They accepted the currently accepted doctrine of predestination as expressed by Thomas à Kempis in his version of *The Imitation of Christ* (q.v.), Book 1, chap. XIII, verse 27. But they felt that the element of personal responsibility must be preserved."

How little the career of Erasmus has meant to many writers of textbooks in the field of world history may be seen in the following section on p. 522 of the present writer's first book in a second edition published by Archon Books: "Equally disappointing is the account in Vol. 1 of the book by Crane Brinton and two colleagues entitled, *A History of Civilization* . . . In the edition of 1955 we read nothing about the Brethren of the Common Life . . . On p. 454 we read this about Erasmus: 'He studied, taught, and lived at Oxford, Cambridge, and Paris, and in Italy, Switzerland, and Germany.' True, he was 'Dutch by birth.' Although he spent the first 25 years of his life in the Netherlands, he studied elsewhere." Although he taught for some years at the University of Louvain, that city is not even mentioned. It is no wonder that in the year 1963 the American Association of University Professors issued a formal report about the courses dealing with the history of civilization. They stated that the situation had become hopeless as the result of poorly organized textbooks. Here are their exact words: "We do not like the course, for it is impossible to teach; it is impossible to maintain a continuity in the course." The Middle Ages were thought to have faded away in a tailspin, especially in the Netherlands, where, according to Henri Pirenne, the renowned Belgian historian, there was a tremendous outburst of commercial and industrial activity, together with a great flowering of art and learning.